A

QUESTION

OF

IDENTITY

Louis Rogers

A Question Of Identity

ISBN-13: 978-1543165425
ISBN-10: 1543165427

Table Of Contents

One   *Questions and assumptions*   7

Two   *Only time will tell*   24

Three   *The eternal and the changeless*   45

Four   *The choice is always ours*   68

Five   *A sense of the sacred*   89

Six   *We should choose wisely*   111

Seven   *Reconstruction begins*   132

Eight   *What are we waiting for?*   153

Nine   *Calming our fears*   174

Ten   *We all belong*   195

Also by Louis Rogers

Coming Alive: Accessing the Healing Power of the Universe
Writer's Club Press, 2000

Mirror of the Unseen: The Complete Discourses of Jalal al-Din Rumi
ToExcel, 2002

The Fire of Love: The Love Story of Layla and Majnun
Writer's Club Press, 2002

Call and Response: The Wisdom of Rumi
iUniverse, 2006

The Age of Spirit
CreateSpace, 2013

Ladder to the Sky
CreateSpace, 2014

Tales of Immortality
CreateSpace, 2015

What Do You Expect God To Be?
CreateSpace, 2015

Where Do We Go From Here?
CreateSpace, 2015

Bridging The Gap
CreateSpace, 2015

Who Do You Think You Are?
CreateSpace, 2015

Kissing The Spider
CreateSpace, 2016

That Which You Wish To Be
CreateSpace, 2016

What Next May Come
CreateSpace, 2016

The Face In The Mirror
CreateSpace, 2016

Rebel In The Mind
CreateSpace, 2016

A Hand In Time
CreateSpace, 2016

As always

For Jennifer, Andrew and Peter

Ashley and Laura

Zoe, Madison and Anna Sophia

And whoever next may come

A Question Of Identity

ONE

Questions and assumptions

Contrary to the way we only assume we understand it, the ego/mind is not a permanent fixture of our spiritual identity, disembodied energy beings that we are in our original nature. Only temporarily embodied in earthly form are we, for the purpose of conscious growth and the enlightenment of the soul. This is who we are. The spirit within, not the body.

The ego/mind is a temporary holding vessel of sorts, containing short-term memories for the soul. Thoughts, feelings, images, sensations, emotions, perceptions and the thousand things that dance in attendance in our memory have been only momentarily captured by our conscious awareness. It is similar in this sense to a software storage device for the ongoing computer programming activities of a computer drive.

Those familiar ideas, images, memories and all other objects of our attention randomly float about in our fields of memory, appearing in our mind's eye for whatever reason they are invoked when recalled back into conscious awareness. They populate the inner world in which we are essentially alone with our thoughts and feelings, with which we identify ourselves and our essential being.

But we are more than that, and we suffer from the limitations of three-dimensional thinking. We allow the physical parameters of material reality to define the ways in which we think, who we think we are, what we think we are and what we are capable of achieving.

We assume so much about the fundamental questions and conventional answers of our existence, never fully realizing that what we take to be self-evident and therefore obvious truths are, on investigation, nothing more than assumptions masquerading as facts.

Our thinking follows along the natural lines of material reality since we physically exist in the material world of natural phenomena. It would appear not only obvious to follow that line of reasoning and experience, but unavoidable.

But it is not. It is an assumption we make instead of direct evidence, or for a supposed lack of evidence to the contrary. We assume we are only physical beings because our physicality is all we consciously know, or so we think. But again, that is only an assumption, surprisingly based on only the extremely limited data that bondage to physical existence alone supplies.

Essentially we are visitors here from a different dimension, the world of spirit, only temporarily embodied in this earthly realm in physical form. The spirit world is not, in this sense, a semi-mythical environment populated by hungry ghosts and angry demons, but a dimension in which consciousness exists in a disembodied state, within energy bodies alone.

Material embodiment being the signature characteristic of this dimension of material manifestation. A hard nut to crack for those who are trying to pierce through the veils of illusion that separate one state from another. A different problem, depending on individual preferences, for those who are not.

Time as well may be experienced differently in physical reality than in the spiritual realm, the non-local field of non-physical reality. Time, as we understand it, may not even exist in any recognizable form in the spirit dimension, the pure energy state of which there may be many different levels of vibrational frequency.

We might even wonder if the mastery of non-dimensional time, if such a thing were conceivable much less possible, would allow for the possibility of traveling through the space/time continuum beyond a strictly linear fashion, as most of us here on the material plane experience it. Are there shortcuts through our linear understanding of the space/time continuum?

If time does not exist in the spirit dimension, why would discarnate entities, those of us who have passed over and those who have transcended the attachment to or need for physical existence, be bound by conventional laws of the space/time continuum?

Might there not be visitations to our reality when the occasion calls for it, and is there not enough widespread evidence from reliable sources that these sort of spiritual anomalies have inflected human history throughout time.

These are question without answers from a conventional scientific or materialistic earthly point of view. There are no conventional assumptions we can invoke to hide behind in our ignorance here, or use to disguise our frustrations at our inability to answer those questions in a meaningful way.

This is where faith helps us make our stand, and faith, for those who are faithful, is often rewarded. By itself not always enough to justify our belief systems, but when accompanied by action, faith can provide the energetic impetus through which our dreams may come true.

All the more reason to turn our attention towards investigating the non-physical nature of our original being, our true existence as spiritual entities. And yet, for some of us we might be wondering what proof there is that any of this is true. In a material realm, what else is to be expected but that we will play by the rules of the conventional game.

Some of us might indeed wonder, and ask questions we do, but too often in the same manner as those who doubted that there was drinkable water over the next ridge, edible food in a near-by valley, and helpful friends waiting to be acknowledged on the other side of the river.

The proof of the pudding is in the eating, so say the rational exegesists with the easy confidence of a gambler with a full house. And sometimes this is true, but sometimes no answers are forthcoming.

If we do nothing about our fears and doubts, questioning nothing for fear of facing increased anxiety and go on about our business as usual, nothing may be all we can reasonably expect. And nothing will come from nothing.

Sometimes the answers to the questions and doubts that arise in our encounters with existence make themselves available, if not consciously known or fully understood. We must make the honest effort to do our own investigation, our own research and seek the answers we hope for with the utmost sincerity and intellectual honesty.

Nothing less than that will do if we are seeking truth. And when the truth we are seeking has to do with our own fundamental being, what other method of self-knowledge would be useful and acceptable.

Only the absolute truth as best we can approach it will serve our interests, no matter what the cost in sentimental attachments to any manufactured past glories whose day has come and gone.

And which still consistently manages to capture our attention, like a favorite movie regularly watched by those who fully lived only in their imagination. As though they preferred living in their imaginary version of the past, ignoring future challenges at their peril, and only-partially alive to the present moment.

So many easy answers are available from so many sources. So many institutions and individuals offering answers and solutions that on closer examination reveal they cannot possibly be authenticated, or results delivered only in accord with the imaginary promises made in their name.

Those kind of pseudo-spiritual bargaining chips and heavenly supplications for earthly purposes are only sad illusions masquerading as history. And all the while a trail of impossible and broken promises left behind litters the landscape of their known histories. What lies beneath the debris field of history may never be known or formally acknowledged.

We search for certitude to the dilemmas of existence, but all too frequently accept answers based solely on short-term memory attention spans. As a culture we seem to be afflicted with this disorder, since the news of the day must always remain only the news of the passing moment. They appear to be cut from the same cloth, but they are not. They are not the same.

That will get us nowhere when we try to deal with serious issues of genuine concern. Serious issues cannot be addressed by easy answers and easy virtue. Those who offer only easy answers are nothing more than salesman selling a product with a limited shelf-life. And those who buy those damaged goods are engaged in an ultimately losing venture with a rapid-fire turn-over of ideas and enthusiasms.

The moment may well be at hand for a serious redress of popular grievances as cultural aspirations begin to fall, one by one, under attack by and under the heel of powerful plutocratic influences. Either aggrieved populations will rise up to accept the burden of self-government in informed and responsible ways, or plutocratic minions will rise to power in the service of their economic overlords.

It would appear that the latter course of events is occurring. Powerful forces, military, religious and economic, always thrive most easily when a general population is divided and unable to act with any effective semblance of group integrity. Things tend to fall apart, and one need only witness the news of the day to see the truth of this in the daily headlines.

Once again, quick and easy answers will have swayed the mass of people who are completely absorbed in the difficult struggles of their lives, unable to devote time, energy or other resources to the larger matters of the day. And as always, looking for a savior of any stripe to rise up out of the ashes of daily existence to point the way to glory.

But the way to glory proposed by self-styled saviors and endorsed by the hungry mob, whose only limits are the limits of free speech, is always accompanied by enormous risk-taking and pitfalls of great depth and hidden dangers.

Scapegoats wearing many-colored apparel are offered up for sacrifice as the reasons for current misfortunes. And blindly endorsed by those who are easily satisfied when complex and confusing times change the familiar landscapes of their lives. They become afraid, filled with doubt and anxiety, and easily swayed by demi-gods posing as saviors.

When nearly-unmanageable change occurs on a daily basis, again and again assumptions rise to popular consciousness and take the place of factual evidence and complex analysis. Easy answers corrupt the integrity of thought itself, resulting not in mature consideration but easy virtue cheaply attained.

This may be when a democracy is slowly and unrecognizably transformed into a plutocracy. Or worse. When entrenched economic and political powers pounce on the opportunity to take overt control over the affairs of a community of people and enslave them.

Only the unconscionably wealthy have the enormous resources to forcibly, although subtly and almost never in direct public sight, inflict their will on others. They are often restless in their heartless and unrelenting search for additional powers, unlimited wealth from unlimited resources, and the complete domination of the environment for their own totalitarian purposes.

Power tends to corrupt and absolute power corrupts absolutely, wrote Lord Acton, described as "the magistrate of history." Lord Acton was one of the great personalities of the nineteenth century, universally considered to be one of the most learned Englishmen of his time. He made the history of liberty his life's work; considering political liberty the essential condition and guardian of religious liberty.

What he passed on through his life and legacy was in the nature of questioning everything, and especially questioning the assumptions we take and mistake for truth, accepting them as the political or other bedrocks of our lives.

It takes immense courage to act on one's own against the mass instincts of a mob mentality bent on maintaining familiar social conventions and traditional thinking in a world of constant change. But each of us, in our own way, is called upon by conscience and duty to do just exactly that.

Not to do that is to stagnate in a morass, if not of our own making, then one which we encourage and empower by our refusal or inability to look more deeply into a matter. And consequently accept in our minds and hearts what we see or are told on the surface level of things.

If we do not question what we are informed is unquestionable authority, the best we can hope for is that we can somehow manage our affairs without sinking under the weight of our misgivings.

But when we give authority too much of the substance they crave, which is power, or they seize it in incremental lots until the power they hold is absolute or nearly so, then once again Lord Acton will be proven to have been prophetically correct.

Not an outcome greatly to be desired, except for those fortunate few who benefit from the tyranny of the powerful and those who suffer from the catastrophic and evolutionarily-regressive effects of diminishing resources and a new age, not of enlightenment, but of economic slavery.

And that would be the rest of us, those of us who cannot afford to insulate ourselves through personal wealth from the crippling effects of disenfranchisement from the security net of social services and communal well-being.

Which may soon well be in the process of undergoing radical dismemberment by those who serve only their personal interests. Those who justify their cruelty, heartless and bigoted as it is, under whatever convenient banner their selfish self-regard is most likely to fly.

The centralization of power and authority in the greedy hands of the greedy few, at the expense of the needy hands of the impoverished many, is the ongoing political and economic misadventure of our time. A world-wide disaster of epic proportions, and a headlong retreat into the stone age of liberal and progressive democracy.

This is the metaphoric devil that has lately come dressed in newer and more expensive clothing, changed and trademarked his name, incorporated the structure of Hell into the fabric of contemporary social concerns. And entered into the very consciousness of the humanity it despises.

As a metaphor, this is not so very far removed from the average everyday experience of the poor among us, the minorities that at lower economic levels function almost as slave-laborers, and those who for one reason or another, any reason really, feel themselves disenfranchised from social traditions and conventional social standards and practices.

A fate which more and more is rapidly becoming a middle-class experience, or what will remain of the middle class when the great social experiment in social services and economic welfare has been destroyed. What now appears to be working well in many progressive European and Scandinavian countries has failed in this country, in which the creator-God has been replaced by the devils of unmanageable industry and unregulated commerce.

And all this power held tightly in the bloody hands of those who reap the profits with a better regard for their own purses than the health and well-being of the country in which they live. And the people they do not serve, but suck-dry for their last few remaining drops of blood. Economic vampires rule the land, and what was once the American dream has become an American nightmare laced with poverty and greed.

Led by false and politically-skewed pseudo-news spread by professional corruption, highlighted with right-wing propaganda, the sheep who do not think themselves sheep blindly and foolishly are led to the slaughter. Convinced by the Quislings among us that they are marching off to victory and bound for glory.

They are not. The concentration camps of poverty and economic slavery no longer need gates and bars on the windows. The harsh and restrictive laws of legally-sanctioned tyranny no longer need armed guards to enforce its dictates.

Harsh though those legal sanctions may be, often cruel and always heartless, only occasionally is physical force needed or invoked. The implied threat of legal action is usually more than enough to change the convictions and opinions of others and subvert their free will. So sheepish are those being led to the slaughter that physical force is rarely called for.

But when it is, stubborn, stupid and brutish stone-age men with stun guns aided by Bronze Age barbarians with water hoses are always at the ready to enforce their masters bidding for thirty pieces of silver, an occasional bone thrown at their feet, and a glancing pat on the back from a mailed fist and a patronizing smile.

This is where we are heading with a socially-conventional practiced smile on our faces, tone-deaf ears to the horrifying underlying realities of our times, and a willful disregard for future probabilities.

The potential pain of them all is too difficult to bear if we encourage it by acknowledging its probable future existence. The suffering may not necessarily be altogether ours, and besides, we are busily engrossed in the immediate details of our everyday lives. They are the brick wall before which we sit.

We are busy. The future will take care of itself, and if it cannot manage by itself we may not be there to experience the shape of things to come anyway. Which we ourselves have had a hand in creating, but then we as well may suffer from the same lack of ability and enthusiasm as those who came before us. The shape of things to come is not necessarily directed by human hands working at fever pitch.

And so it goes. Always putting off until the morrow what is too damn hard to do today, a policy of social and political expediency that in the long run has never proven to be a particularly useful social and political expediency that can endure over a long haul.

Damaging and destructful as this is in the arena of average every-day human affairs, when it comes to our spiritual interests and the transformational processes of human nature, it is chaos itself.

Chaos may one day erupt into meaningful momentum in a specific direction, but the impulse towards order cannot be proven to emerge out of the inchoate energies of chaotic interference.

Surely one would suspect that some outside influence may have been brought to bear, rather than an emergent force ordering itself from within itself, and thereby inflecting its particular template in the reality of which it is a part.

There is a well-known pseudo-scientific paradox some of us contemplate with the same attention and interest as Zen practitioners contemplate a Zen koan. Simply stated, it asks what happens when an irresistible force encounters an immoveable object?

It is an impossible question to answer because it postulates an impossible situation. If a universe exists in which there is an irresistible force, that means it would be impossible for an immoveable object to exist in the same reality. The existence of one would deny the possibility of the other.

And the reverse would also be true. If a universe exists in which there is an immoveable object, that means there cannot possibly exist an irresistible force in that same reality or it would not be defined as an immoveable object.

Again, the existence of one would deny the existence of the other if we suggest they occupy the same reality. Therefore the answer to the question is not in the standard form we might expect, and over which we might wrack our brains in a futile attempt to answer the question. To take it literally would be like trying to solve a Zen koan through linear logic.

The only answer is that the question is without meaning since there cannot be a cross-over from one reality to another, from a reality in which an irresistible force exists to a reality in which there is an immoveable object.

But could there be a cross over from the spiritual dimension to this reality? Those who profess religious faith must say yes to this question, since the existence of religion itself supposedly testifies to this cross-over.

The existence of holy beings in every religious tradition testifies that human consciousness can be directly influenced and affected by the spiritual realm. And what else are prayers, supplications, rites and rituals for but the very human attempt to influence the spiritual realm to act favorably and directly in human affairs?

Can a conscious cross-over occur, that is to say, can the human mind be conscious of the spiritual realm and act in both or in tandem? For that is the purpose of all traditions that teach methods for the transformation of human consciousness, to expand the boundaries of awareness.

The result being a transformed consciousness, an enlightened mind, a being capable of representing through his or her sayings and doings the presence of the divine radiation in human affairs. The meaning of genuine sainthood, holy beings and spiritual mastery.

Spiritual mastery does not imply foolish and self-serving claims to authority over the spiritual domain, it suggests mastery of the functional processes of the human mind to such an extent that one is able to go beyond the traditional activities of the ego/mind to pierce through the depths of human consciousness and enter the realm of spirit

The domain of spirit lies within the human frame. The spiritual master has entered into the subterranean complexities of consciousness itself, explored the creative energies of the cosmos, and entered the realm of God on the earthly plane. The spiritual master has become enlightened to the God-presence within.

Why temper our spiritual ambitions with uneasy allegiances to ancient doctrines and Bronze Age theologies when so much more awaits us in the human adventure. The past is not meant to be our future, unless we lack the courage to move beyond the self-restrictive borders of our fears.

Some of us may have no genuine spiritual convictions based on our common humanity. Or of the reality of the spirit realm that informs us beyond the standard religious teachings we once were taught when we were children.

Our relative ignorance in these matters of present and futuristic concern will present a standard barrier that must be deeply penetrated before we can enlighten ourselves to the true nature and spiritual potential of mankind.

It cannot be an evolutionary goal to content ourselves with reciting ancient litanies in tandem. Or chant medieval psalms in candle-lit halls with accompanying choirs simulating an imaginary heavenly chorus.

Our spiritual goal must be to find within ourselves what it is we are really searching for when we look through the prisms of our affairs for the window to our soul. The source of being seems so much more in line with our evolutionary destiny than the window dressings with which we decorate our spirit. It seems right to do so because it *is* right.

To argue against that is simply to waste time reinforcing ancient prejudices, but having nothing to do with the state of our current spiritual well-being and future progress in that direction.

Nor would it increase our real happiness, the depth of our self-knowledge, and a secure sense that we are heading for a bright future with genuine potential for an enhanced fullness of being.

We cannot continue to exist in a state of competitive hostility, fighting each other over rapidly diminishing natural resources. Nor indulge our failed institutional insistence in a perpetual state of spiritual self-loathing based on some imaginary original sin.

Myths are not factual events. They do not describe actual occurrences to which we must subscribe as historical narratives. Myths are not history, they are psychological and spiritually derived teachings which may be useful for the people for whom they were created.

But which may not prove useful for latter generations, who might mistake the glue that holds those stories together for the hard and fast concrete of a construction site in Hell.

Which is why so many of those ancient stories fall apart on closer examination, or disintegrate over time.

Myths are constructed over time, but not necessarily from divine revelation. They should always be closely examined for what they bring to light in modern sensibilities. Therefore we should choose, and choose carefully, before we order our existence around the shadowy details of what a long-dead civilization structured as the central facts of their lives.

Everything changes over time, and considering the relatively brief span of a human lifetime, we ought to be intimately familiar with the inevitable processes of change. Which ought to make us thoughtful and selective concerning what we accept into our circle of belief.

The ongoing activities of change which characterize mortal existence tend only to engulf us in the fruitless search for certitude. And in our relative ignorance of the universe and how it works, any such belief in permanence is doomed from the start to a premature burial.

Each age must seek its own salvation, and each succeeding generation must build anew on the bones of its forefathers. We can never be satisfied with or accept for ourselves what previous ages have thought as our own experience. The problems of yesterday are not the same issues that face us today, although in a larger sense every age must find a way to deal with the pressing problems of human existence.

We can admire past achievements and build on them, but this is an incredibly vast universe, far beyond our ability to conceptualize, and a largely unknown reality in which we live.

To continue believing in any ancient myth that casts us all in the role of sinners, tainted with the imaginary stain of original sin is to willfully cast a shadow over our essential nature as being corrupted by an event that never was or ever could have been.

Imagine believing in a talking snake, as though it was actual history and not simply the fevered imagination of ancient peoples at work in the vain attempt to explain human suffering and misery as the work of a demonic being.

This may absolve the more naïve among us of the guilt associated with human misdeeds by casting a wider net and snaring a world of devils and demons in it. But it hardly passes the tests of reason and enlightened thinking.

And who among us now really believes that story is worthy of thoughtful consideration, much less affecting our belief system such that we live under the shadow of a demonic presence among us. This is the ongoing problem of mistaking myth as history and misinterpreting the resulting confusion.

We are not casting out demons when we attempt to exorcize our mythic-minded imaginations with expensive rites and high-minded rituals, we are merely throwing away our money and wasting time and energy in the process.

We are bound to no one and nothing in our search for closure, except to the truth. Compromise will get us nothing and nowhere if we accept as truth what in our hearts we do not truly believe.

Or pay lip service with our minds and bodies to established norms of conventional thought and traditional beliefs. This is inauthentic to our inner being.

When we know in our hearts that we are merely doing so out of convenience and for the sake of social acceptance, we make a farce out of any supposed advanced enterprise in spiritual awareness. And making us hypocrites in the process.

Something we can ill afford to do now, when our world and supposed civilization is entering such advanced states of physical, moral and spiritual decay. Things are falling apart, and anyone with eyes to see and ears to hear can find the evidence for themselves.

A critical read through the daily newspapers, or a few hours spent on the Internet will quickly reveal a world in serious and potentially terminal disarray. World-wide communication is nearly instantaneous now because of the various forms of media information easily available to anyone with a cell phone or Internet access.

Bad news can no longer be quietly swept under the rug as was once possible when information was easily controlled by dictatorial central authorities. A world in which anyone revealing state secrets of any degree of seriousness was quickly punished, and damaging information hidden from public view. Freedom of any sort is always in danger, always susceptible to infringement of one sort or another.

Not that organized institutional authorities are still not trying to control what the mass of men think and do, but that the world-wide spread of means and methods of dissimulating and receiving information are fast outgrowing traditional methods of control and censorship.

Information is now available from highly-informed sources that enable us to think for ourselves and formulate opinions based on solid evidence. If, that is, we have the courage and intention to do so and take our future in our own hands.

If we are willing to make the effort, that is what we will do. If we are not willing to make the effort and resist the empowerment that comes with informed opinion, we will progress no further that the emotional resistance that dominates our thinking and retards all forward movement.

What we will individually do is a matter of conscience, but as a collective race of sentient beings we seem most content when we allow others to inform us and shape the content of our collective future. And there are always those ready to do just exactly that as they make their bid for power.

This cannot be allowed to continue as long as the warnings of Lord Acton concerning the abuse of power still holds true for our species. And his insights still appear to reflect the general condition of humanity, with which we must still actively contend until we somehow jump-start our own evolution.

Perhaps the Internet and easy Internet access is the means by which we will do that. It may be that the only way to overcome the lethargy and inertia of a generally drugged and pacified group consciousness is through force-feeding humanity information that will so excite the collective imagination that it may overcome the spiritual sloth of contemporary existence. Only time will tell, and only determined planning along enlightened lines of thought and action will make it so.

Two

Only time will tell

We live in an age of information, which also means we live in an age of communication. What kind of information is communicated may be a major problem, as well as the many ways in which we communicate with each other.

How both or either can be polluted by various forms of censorship and institutional control is another serious issue, as is our ability to detect when we are falsely informed about serious issues that are vital to our general health and our intellectual and moral well-being.

Our very freedom is at stake when information is censored to favor the few and place the many at a disadvantage. As are our inalienable liberties threatened when our access to truth is denied or compromised.

We may believe we are free as we continue to labor blindly in the orchards of ignorance under the patronizing flag of institutional authority. But if we are laboring under false ideas and incomplete or seriously-edited information, our ability to undertake meaningful action will be, *and generally is,* severely curtailed.

True freedom lies in knowing the truth of any situation, and the ability to act on our own perceptions and individual reactions to the world around us. With no authority to control us other than our own good conscience, and a mind informed by accurate information, reasonable methods of inquiry and rational means of judgement and discourse. Along with a determined effort to act in fairness and honesty.

This is hard work for those willing to work hard, but impossible standards to meet for those who are not. Which one we are is a matter of individual choice and ability, but which one we are will inevitably help to determine the shape and content of our individual futures.

As a collective race of self-conscious beings, we will inevitably suffer from whatever fate the collective weight of our wisdom or foolishness influences the pendulum of time that holds sway over our destiny.

The weight of our collective ignorance or enlightenment will influence that hanging pendulum to remain in the darkness of stagnation or move towards the light. Individually we will move forward according to our own momentum, but collectively we appear to be bound by whatever social, political and religious restrictions or freedoms we enjoy.

As individuals we may enjoy a fuller expression of freedom than we do as members of a community of socially-oriented, institutionally-allied and therefore potentially mortgaged bond-slaves or day-laborers. There may well be advantages in either situation, but there are disadvantages as well.

To pursue the freedom of our own choices and consequent beliefs is to risk our social approbation. If within the interior expansion of self-knowledge and self-identification we take exception to conventional beliefs, we may find ourselves with no choice but to avoid culturally well-traveled roads on our journey through rugged terrain and the inner landscape of our psyche. The journey to enlightenment is always within.

We may find ourselves intellectually and spiritually on our own, which also suggests that a fair amount of discretion will be necessary if we live in a community of conventional individuals. We may wish to speak the truth of our researches and discoveries, but if we live in a repressive environment and judgmental society, not too far and not too loud.

"Do not give what is holy to the dogs; nor cast your pearls before swine, lest they trample them under their feet, and turn and tear you in pieces." Mathew 7:6.

There may always be those who will resist or resent any change in thinking that comes their way. And who find it necessary, if not imperative, to act on their resistance to the detriment of the individual freedoms and liberties of others, which they may deem necessary to protect and preserve their own vested interests. When that happens they are acting out of fear not love, which within religious boundaries always violates the spirit of the divine encounter.

The kind of thinking that leads to extremism, which cannot be for the common good by definition since it admits no alternatives to its totalitarian world view. Freedom is always at risk when extremists seek power, and liberty can never be taken for granted when they gain control of anything.

The power of those words cannot be energized only from an ancient scroll or modern declaration. It can only be activated when the hearts and minds of men and women are united in common cause, and actively resist the threats that power-hungry individuals and institutions potentially threaten us with when they seek to assert their dominance.

Our freedom to explore our essential being is always in jeopardy when it suggests to powerful forces that we are unwilling to remain anesthetized sheep in the general course of events.

The more we learn about ourselves and others, the more we will begin to realize that we are all in the same collective boat, and that it has aged and is leaking on all sides. So many things in which we once believed and committed to with absolute certainty have undergone serious scrutiny and reevaluation in recent years, and have emerged absolutely the worse for wear.

This is a serious cultural threat to our sense of religious health and well-being, and because of the presence of the Internet to fuel the discussion, cannot be hushed by clerical sanctions or swept under an ecclesiastical rug.

Nor can any genuine sense of spiritually-enlightened well-being be legislated into existence under the rubric of some imaginary defense of freedom, called into existence through repressive and regressive laws, legal restriction or declarations of national holidays celebrating what is nothing more than some particular or group of legislator's personal preferences.

Our national Declaration of Independence is more than simply a political document justifying our separation from an unresponsive and repressive ruling power. It is a statement of our inalienable rights and the recourse to which we have access when those rights are consistently violated.

Our political rights were detailed in that Declaration and established in our Constitution, but our spiritual rights have been violated for a very long period of time now. They are inviolate, but not according to entrenched institutional authorities, social zealots and political extremists.

This is a far-cry from the historically-accurate original intentions of the framers of the constitution. And even further afield from the true purpose of any genuine spiritual tradition.

The goal of human activity is clearly progress in exploring and understanding advanced levels of the space/time continuum, achieving a secure level of comfort and safety on the material plane. And illuminating the mind of man through increasing complex, accurate and informing levels of information and experience.

But the goal of human existence is more significantly the enlightenment of the spirit, not the militant control of the mind nor the economic enslavement of the body that is fast becoming a standard barrier that must be penetrated by discerning minds.

We are fast exhibiting mythic lemming-like behavior on a massive scale following the lead of a vast array of would-be leaders who act only in their own interests. This is something that has never before*recorded by history on such a world-wide and massive field of battle. *been*

The biblical injunction enjoining stewardship of the planet on man has ultimately degenerated in modern times into an economically-inspired motivation to despoil the planet for financial gain and the exploitation of natural resources. Forgetful, as those despoilers are, that we have nowhere else to go and no place else to live. We are fouling our own nest.

And we, passive onlookers that so many of us are, have become enablers of that destruction through our refusal to join forces and fight back against the rape of the environment.

Our general unwillingness or inability to face these issues may seal our fate as we face the potentially oncoming destruction that may, one day in the not too far off distant future, send us all scurrying back to the caves and foraging for food, warmth and drinkable water.

This is obvious to anyone who pays attention, but so serious is the problem that it cannot be repeated enough until it breaks through the sealed barriers of the average mind entombed in its own affairs.

There must be a resurgence of hope in the nobility of the human experiment and our rightful place in the cosmos as children of the universe. And offspring of the universal intelligence that has devised the creation.

Not as a dictatorial controlling authority with merciless rules and a general indifference to our individual fate and collective well-being, but as the source behind the façade of material manifestation. To which we, conscious, sentient, self-aware and self-activating offspring of the universe that we are, are in direct relationship to that infinite spirit.

Call it the infinite, inchoate field of organizing intelligence, God, infinite spirit, source or anything one can imagine, but the reality is we swim like otters in the sea of God, within the infinite energy fields of infinite spirit, in a universe of consciousness characterized by bliss and ennobled by love.

Call our existence an act of unmotivated grace, grateful that our origins are found in a grand plan of universal design rather than a random accident of recombinant energies and fortuitous chemical combinations that somehow produced life and conscious, self-aware existence.

Science may explain the resulting processes, but the origins remain a mystery, no matter how cleverly that ignorance is disguised. To believe either explanation, accidental birth or grand design, clearly requires an enormous leap of faith. But which alternative is most satisfying to the needs of our soul and the demands of our spirit is the question upon which our identity rests.

Which of these options, we may ask ourselves, has the greatest potential for inner illumination. The way of science, which seeks proof of our existence through experimentation with external phenomena. Or the way of spirit, which seeks to find within our own consciousness the source of being for which we need no instrumentation other than the penetrating insight of an enlightened mind.

Those who advance into matured old age understand clearly the ephemeral nature of physical existence, which those enjoying their younger years are unable to feel with the same assurety that they still feel in their youth.

Because of that and so many other extraordinarily important signature features of mortal existence, we must learn how to accelerate our evolution before we bring disaster down upon ourselves through the misuse of technology and our poor stewardship and destruction of the environment.

Isn't it more than obvious now that we can no longer afford to indulge the general immaturity and corrupt leadership of those who are essentially untrained for positions of power, authority and high responsibility.

The planet is suffering and we along with it. As are all natural features of the planetary landscape, and all other life forms with which we share and enjoy this extraordinary world of enormous beauty and womb-like features that birth an extraordinary variety of seedlings.

In an odd sort of way, we are collectively the universal mind in search of itself, just as we ourselves mirror that endeavor as we search within our fundamental being for our own separate identities throughout the whole of our lives. It all apparently rests on a question of identity.

This is the riddle to be solved as we stumble our way through the accumulated debris fields of world and personal history. Wisdom here is of the greatest and most serious regard as we separate the spiritual wheat from the earthly chaff.

We are after truth, the whole truth and nothing but the truth as is commonly maintained. The difficulties of which may have escaped our attention as some of us naively assumed that as we are, and without advanced training in spiritual traditions and beliefs, we have the knowledge, insight and perception to accomplish so formidable a task on our own and without informed guidance.

But what choice do we have except to face the challenges of existence and do our best to solve the riddle of the Sphinx as it shape-shifts into our individual lives. Or if not, fall back into the sleep of unconsciousness which characterizes so much of our waking hours. Perhaps waking dreams might be a more accurate way of describing the dream state we mistake for reality, or so say spiritual teachers with the clearest insights into the spiritual realm.

In that regard we may eventually find we are essentially innocent, unsophisticated, artless, ingenuous, inexperienced, guileless, unworldly and trusting in our own mistaken perceptions of our world and the universe in which we have our apparent being.

Most of us seemingly trust only in the evidence of our physical senses, which belongs to the lower levels of judging the world. And yet our senses misjudge reality in so many ways, as has been demonstrated many times in many ways in well-known scientific experiments.

We should pay serious attention to the assumptions we unconsciously and automatically make about the reliability of our physical senses, for upon that often unreliable evidence we judge the world, ourselves and our place in reality.

And as we examine our minds and the contents of our consciousness, we assume that our inner selves are the same as the contents of the inner library in which we have stocked our ever-growing shelves of books, magazines, video tapes, CDs and the assorted methods of storing and retrieving information with which we entertain and enervate our spirit.

What an assumption that is, and what an error. Upon that internal morass of relevant and irrelevant information we retreat into our personal fortress of solitude. But it is a grave mistake and a headlong retreat into dreams and illusions. And when we do that we are creating an imaginary edifice built on quicksand.

No sooner do we make a new assumption about our existence, convinced that we have arrived at certitude, then we discover that we have only prematurely closed our accounts with reality. There is always more to come.

And that precariously incomplete state of self-knowledge is forced to undergo a premature burial in the manner of the great misadventures of human history.

An error we will endlessly repeat, time after time, lifetime after lifetime, until we finally recognize that we are judging ourselves only according to the mind's limited state of inner perceptions and the wrapping paper they arrive in.

The mind can never know itself; it can only know the contents of its consciousness. And we are definitely not that, not the contents, nor are we the packaging in which it is wrapped. We are not the objects of our attention even though they seemingly fill our awareness when we focus our gaze on them and the outside world.

They, the things we see, and hear, and do and think are not the truths that compromise our identity. They are only the objects of our awareness, and when we take them in and store them in the inner warehouse of memory they become only the contents of our consciousness.

But none of that was there when we were newly-born and wrapped in swaddling clothes. And yet there we were, foaming at the mouth and eager to get on with the experience of life, but incomplete, inexperienced and inept. Children waiting for their second birth into the realities of the world we were. It takes time to get on with things.

As time passes we do get on with it. And after enough time has passed eventually becoming forgetful that we are all visitors to a small planet on this material plane. We are here for the physical and mental adventure, along with the essential education of the spirit.

We are not here through some fortuitous but random accident of chemical recombinations in which chance mutations may have had a hand in the assumed accidental design of the human body. But those who think along these lines are incorrect in their assumptions, which very likely also deny the existence of an immortal soul. They are perhaps uneducated in matters of the spirit, and perhaps unwilling as well to accept the challenge it poses.

When our time here has ended we will have no choice but to leave behind all the treasures and souvenirs some of us may have spent a lifetime collecting, and to which we adhere with the passion of a lifetime's obsession. To what ultimate end, and for what purpose the accumulation of goods.

In the end life is a dream, a play of consciousness. If we forget that we may well believe instead in the illusions we have created for the entertainment of our own self-interest and those we cherish. Including those as well who empower the illusions of our inner world.

We may never awaken from the waking dream we imagined was life if we are content to remain oblivious to these basic and fundamental truths of human existence.

Spiritual traditions take an opposite tack, imploring us to awaken from the waking dream of forgetfulness, encouraging us to follow their well-developed techniques for the remembrance, self-recognition and self-realization of our true nature.

If we are satisfied with the way things are, happy in our material existence as it is, uninterested in what may follow and what it is within our essential nature of which we may be unaware, we will pay no attention to the inner prompting of our restless souls. We will not heed the call of spirit.

Our inner cell phone may ring at all hours of the day or night but the call will go unanswered. Whether deliberately or inadvertently through negligence, we often miss the opportunities to expand our consciousness that come our way. And the suffering continues by whatever name we identify it.

Perhaps it is a matter of expanding our belief system first before we can begin to expand our consciousness. First have the belief, as has often been taught, then experiences will follow. We should learn how to listen to that sage advice.

What kinds of experiences are suggested? An answer that satisfies one person may in all likelihood be unsatisfactory to another. We are all so very different in so many ways that it is all but impossible to suggest a simple answer to a very complicated and often painful problem.

There is an impersonal answer, which is not to anticipate that the call of spirit will appear in a pre-formulated, conventional manner. Contrary to formal expectations, spirit will not be bound by traditional formulations according to individual or institutional pre-conceptions.

How the underlying intelligence of the universe should respond to the human dilemma is an individual affair. To do otherwise and travel a common road is simply to seek answers in the mirror of human affairs that time provides, but it is only a backwards glance into history.

This is not to suggest that the spiritual realm is unaware of human suffering or indifferent to individual fate, but it does imply that the greater cannot be known by the lesser. The part can never know the whole.

We stand before the mystery of existence naked and afraid, but our fear and impotence is not enough to justify the premature conclusions which too many of us may have already drawn. And which have generally lost the power to inform.

Who are we to question the creative intelligence that has fashioned the universe in such an extraordinary manner. The fact that we all experience suffering does not automatically suggest the universe is callous or indifferent.

There is no reliable evidence in that regard, beyond the fact that mortal existence involves suffering, that spirit is unyielding to the needs of its children and its creation.

Suffering is an essential element of duality, and we exist on the earthly plane of material duality. For every action there is an equal and opposite reaction. Where there is fear there is also love. Where there is sorrow there is happiness as well. Where pain exists so also is there the joy of existence. And where there is suffering there is also the ecstasy of life.

Beneath the surface appearance of things is the unmotivated bliss which is the true nature of consciousness. We are told by those who know, the spiritual masters of mankind, that bliss is the essential nature of consciousness.

Pure consciousness is one without a second, which means there is no duality in the infinite field of bliss. This cannot be repeated enough, only until it ultimately pierces through to our central core of beliefs and inflects our consciousness.

Nothing exists that can threaten the essential bliss of consciousness when it recognizes itself as such. And that is the empowerment of a spiritual tradition, to help us regain that missing knowledge, the truest quest of the human condition.

We are that for which we seek elsewhere, our uncertainty about our own being leading us to premature conclusions. Which is that we can find through some external source what we assume is missing in our own nature. Again, the foolishness of immature and unexplored assumptions.

If we do nothing concerning the fulfilment of our spiritual concerns and well-being, accepting only the evidence of our senses and the premature conclusions of an untrained and inexperienced mind, we will stagnate in a morass of our own making.

This is generally untrue of most other fields of the human experience. But when it comes to the essential nature of consciousness we are often content to beg the issue and head off in different directions, all of which assure the continued safety and security of our ego and the internal structures in consciousness it has created and maintained.

Most of which will very likely lead nowhere and no place but to a nearly infinite regress of opportunities. The call of spirit may come to each of us in its own way and ours. But go unrecognized when we have no template or model with which to consult.

Once again we will have squandered an opportunity to expand our consciousness into formerly unchartered territories and realms of being. We can never know this for certain without that direct experience of spiritual encounter, but it is only our failure of nerve and lack of spiritual courage that holds us back from that infinite adventure.

We may have spiritual beliefs, but we may also lack the courage of conviction. Perhaps conviction is an issue we might look into with genuine attention and perseverance. We may believe in the spiritual domain, but if we are not fully convinced of its existence and its rightful place in our lives we will make no progress in achieving illumination.

Without genuine experience of the spiritual realm our spiritual convictions will lack depth and complexity. We cannot make real progress surfing only on the surface waves of sentimental attachments and half-hearted belief systems.

We must go much deeper into the fundamental nature of life to find and experience those inner truths for ourselves. Direct experience is the best teacher. Not the only teacher by any means, but by far the best because of its power to affect the perceptions that have stagnated in our awareness.

A genuine experience of our inner existence can inflect our consciousness in the direction of truth. This is greatly to be desired if our soul is troubled, and we are aware that something of genuine substance and sustenance is missing in our lives.

It may be a vague feeling of dissatisfaction, or it may come like an unexpected tsunami of powerful feelings that threatens to engulf our inner being and submerge us in a sea of troubles.

But this might very well be the call of spirit that some us wait for with baited breaths, but which we mistake simply as the effects of the misfortunes in life we all endure in one form or another. The call of spirit can come as a call to change whatever it is that needs to be changed.

Perhaps we hear the call of spirit most clearly, in a lower state of being, when we are open and vulnerable because life's misadventures have inflected our awareness. A conspicuous time in an odd but informing way, when we are most willing to actualize the experience of a call to higher realms of spirit. Who can know for certain how and when this occurs, except a spiritual master adept in the ways of spiritual demeanor.

The difficulty many of us face in confronting the spiritually-unknown lies in knowing what to believe and in whom we can place our trust. If we rely on the thinking process alone we will always require proof for our adopted beliefs unless we are ruled by our emotional nature. But which nevertheless can often be unreliable and frequently self-deceiving.

Trust is a key issue, but there are aspects of our lives that we automatically believe offer us some measure of security in the daily and routine matters of our existence. There are biological matters which we affirm and fulfill as best we can because we adhere to their principles as fundamental laws of nature.

When we do that we follow the way of natural law, an essential principle of existence that affirms our right to life. Since those laws rule our existence without the mind interfering and necessitating an internal debate about the path we must follow. Or placating an imaginary deity out of religious fear or existential panic, whatever follows may well be a matter of interpretation.

We breathe, we eat, we adhere to the biological imperatives that flow through our being and dominate our automatic reflexes. We learn to trust those instincts, having nowhere else to go for confirmation because they are our genetic inheritance. And clearly, this is the way of nature.

But there are spiritual instincts within us as well, and it would be well for us to consider the source of those instincts as an additional genetic inheritance. Along with the clarity of purpose which they unveil, and which we follow when we are at our best and allow the dictates of the heart to predominate over our thinking.

Those instincts are mirrored in our awareness through the spiritual questions that arise unbidden and unedited in our minds. Is there meaning in life, they demand. Is there order, purpose, a design of sorts in which we have a rightful place.

What is the source of life, where have we come from, where are we going, and is there a meaningful direction towards which we should bend our efforts. What lies behind the appearance of the universe.

All cultures and civilizations have faced these fundamental questions about life, and few things survive of any particular value when those cultures eventually depart from the scene. Aside from whatever relics furnish forth the museums, estates, antique shops and treasure houses of racial memory.

What does survive of more than ephemeral value is when we have either tried or found a way to put ourselves in accord with universal principles of existence. And it is those active principles of existence that give the individual life force the spiritual meaning for its existence.

This is necessary to align the believing soul in accord with the immediate culture, the world, the reigning deity and the universe which contains them all.

Most cultures have affirmed the existence of a creator or a creative force, and all who do have established methods for accessing the inherent wisdom of any divine revelations in which they believe and to which they have access.

Most cultures do not choose to go through life without some form of recourse to spirit, or deny the existence of a creative intelligence behind the universe. There is no evidence of any civilization based completely on atheistic beliefs. Individuals may, but cultures generally do not take on that burden unless they are ruled by totalitarian overlords.

Other than those under the firm rule of religious repressionists, relatively few willingly assume that we are alone and on our own in the universe. And that when death comes we take our final bow and make our exit with no possibility of a return visit.

Such a negative and pessimistic view of existence is antithetical to productive social order and psychological well-being. Ultimately it is harmful to the human spirit, and has consequently never been a particularly popular approach.

Death is a curtain call relatively few of us are particularly anxious to take. And even fewer are educated in the course of events that inevitably follow on the death of the body.

A highly debatable and controversial issue, although the fact of death is so frightening to so many of us that any serious discussion involving different points of view is hardly likely to draw an enthusiastic and attentive audience.

Fear of death has a tendency to infringe on our love of life. It overshadows all our activities as we age and begin to feel the slow and steady disintegration of the body. This is seemingly inevitable in this realm of duality, that love will inevitably be shadowed by its dualistic opposite, fear.

Fear is a legitimate experience, which cannot be denied. But to fear something we do not understand seems like another in an endless series of assumptions that plague humanity.

Better to understand what we consciously or unconsciously fear than live in fear of what we do not understand. And are not willing to make the serious attempt to investigate, held back by the unknown fears we cannot properly define.

Fear makes cowards of us all, holding us in perpetual hostage to life's imponderables and the consequences of embodied existence. But death is the necessary ending for the continuous cycle of growth, maturity and decline. New life begins where the old leaves off, and that is the inescapable reality of embodied existence.

Material form is always undergoing the processes of change, and death one more step in the sequential processes of life. Small consolation if we identify ourselves only as physical beings, which is so much the cause of our mental suffering and existential anxieties.

The question of identity must be resolved in order to escape the consequences of our ignorance and confusion in the matter. There is no escaping the essential fact that we will all continue to suffer as long as we continue to live with the unsolved mysteries of life and death.

In this regard, fear is the inevitable result of the confusion of identity that inflects our understanding of existence, and tempers our regard for the seemingly unbearable inevitabilities of physical existence.

Physical existence is not an easy or predictable affair. There is no security, and as is obvious, no one gets out of it alive. But that depends on how we define existence, and what we regard as the true measure of our personal identity.

Are we simply mortal beings, doomed to personal extinction when the death of the physical body occurs as skeptics and material reductionists apparently believe, but often against their personal will and best hopes for any future existence.

Or are we immortal beings, infinite and immortal consciousness experiencing physical embodiment for purposes of evolutionary growth along lines of spiritual maturity. Which sounds much more like a best-case scenario than material reductionists might be willing to accept.

What choice we make and what we believe will necessarily determine the extent to which fear rules over our responses to whatever confronts us along the way. Self-identity and self-knowledge will most likely determine our spiritual and philosophical fate.

Under which powerful influence will we experience this material existence, and under whose sway will our deepest and most closely-held beliefs shade our daily existence?

We always need to get on with the business of life. But ridding ourselves of the phantom spectre of death, if indeed it is true, as spiritual teachings claim, that consciousness never dies is a genuinely useful step in acknowledging our immortal existence. And thereby adding quality to our psychological and spiritual state of mind.

This puts an entirely different accent on our understanding of existence, and may ease the burden that fear of physical death takes on our spirit. Those who claim that this is merely self-deception and delusionary thinking might well be advised to refresh their understanding of what a genuine spiritual teaching has to offer.

And then inform themselves even further through the experiences of advanced practitioners and adepts as well, with first-hand accounts concerning the effects of the teachings on individual lives.

And the probable reasons the teachings have continued to survive in spite of harsh intellectual reactionaries, a hostile institutional climate, and the physical hardships of this world. They survive in a world often overtly hostile to enlightened teachers and mystical teachings.

Especially since those teachers and teachings concern the evolution and transformation of consciousness, which can neither effectively be controlled by legislation nor contained by shunning the teachers and banning the teachings.

Genuine mystical teachings will always survive because spirit is eternal, far stronger than whatever the merely temporal political or religious climate is interested in censoring for their own shallow purposes

We are naturally far more than simply attached to our bodies. We do everything we can to ensure our continued health and well-being. Age and the shadow that illness casts over our being do nothing to ease that continuous psychological burden.

And in extreme cases, death may be a palliative relief when physical suffering becomes intense. For those of us in so desperate a situation, death may be something in the nature of a welcome friend.

But for the rest of us, not quite yet. To finally recognize the true nature of our immortal existence and the temporary nature of our physical embodiment will go a long way towards helping us overcome the limitations of our traditional assumptions about life and future bearing. And the manner in which we choose to live our lives.

And very possibly begin the serious and solemn exploration of the spiritual nature of our being. We may finally find ourselves paying serious attention to the teachings and techniques spiritual traditions have developed in their ongoing devotions to the revelation and realization of our infinite and eternal nature.

The thought of death so terrifies the ego-mind and untrained conscious awareness that we are deeply hampered by mortal fears, often unable to effectively respond to future possibilities.

More than that, it gives free rein to the unenlightened mind to seek only after its own interests, heedless that there will indeed be consequences. And with that, the realization that this life is only part of a much larger process of existence. That whatever we do here will have accumulating effects for which we will have to account at some future time. The universal law of karma must always be addressed.

If not in this life then in the next. And if not then, then the next, or the next, or the one after that. However long it takes, we are all ultimately destined to rejoin the source of being. But not as the imperfect beings most of us know ourselves to be, for in that imperfection lie the seeds of doubt and discord.

Whatever those individuated needs and desires are, they are what prevent us from experiencing conscious reunion with source. The impulse towards separation and individuation creates in us a compulsive need to go our own way. To experience for ourselves and in our own individual way the manifestation of a separate inner reality in which we reign rather than serve. A misguided notion, for when we rejoin the whole we have everything to gain and nothing to lose except our illusions.

A separate reality will be inevitable if separation occurs only to serve the needs of the ego. But at some point we can effectively learn to see through the archetypical responses that ego creates in response to life and whatever situations are brought to bear on us.

We can learn to see through those predictable and self-serving responses, and seeing through them we obviate the need to serve them. In overcoming them we also outgrow the former self that once we were. We evolve, grow and mature.

There is something greater within us we can serve with honor and distinction. Instead of continually mistaking the ego's reactions and demands as a reflection of true being, we can search within ourselves for the deepest truth of our existence. All of which exist far below the surface level of attention in which the ego rules.

Why would we want to go beyond the likes and dislikes, the preferences and desires that rule our conscious thinking and perennial attention. Why would we want to abandon our habitual ways of thinking and behaving in favor of something to which we may or may not have conscious access.

The answer is that those preference and desires are not true being, they are merely habits we have established in life to which we subscribe for want of a better and more spiritually informing alternative.

And so we remain at the inevitably disintegrating level of comfort and security we are best able to maintain, and in that process risk stagnation in our conscious evolution. For some of us this is the way things are. Others hold out the hope that things will improve, and eventually allow them to get on with the consciously evolving nature of their being without serious effort, as an act of grace.

There are others among us who actively work to expand and deepen their awareness of being; to excavate through the depths of their psyche. To reach and experience within the fundamental and universal stratum of consciousness the true and ultimate nature of being.

Those are the brave pioneers of the inner life, who risk the safety and security of everything most of us traditionally hold firmly in our conscious attention. All in hopes of attaining that which is beyond the conventional assumptions that can merely be held within the surface levels of our attention, and are therefore susceptible to change. What they seek is the eternal and the changeless. And so should we.

THREE

The eternal and the changeless

In a sense, the persistent refusal to deny or consciously avoid our spiritual nature and live only according to the instincts of the body and the fleeting vagaries of the mind is a descent into temporal madness.

Frustrating this is, sad beyond dispute, and an unhappy observation of the manner in which so many of us have come perilously close to stalling on the material plane of our evolutionary journey.

If not actually overstepping the bounds of evolutionary propriety in the manner of holocaust or climate deniers, evolutionary reactionaries among us cling to a worn-out insistence that physical reality is all that is and all that can be experienced. The proof of that particular pudding is still up for grabs, an assumption masquerading as fact.

In this extraordinary universe of wonders without end, the compulsive-obsessive insistence and primary recourse only on evidence from the physical senses and material experimentation alone in exploring our inner and outer environment is nearly child-like in the elementary nature of those investigations.

If not completely insensitive to the inner promptings that all of us experience from time to time, our over-reliance on physicality seemingly conflicts with our religious beliefs that we are essentially spiritual beings embedded in temporary material forms.

This is a paradox not easily overcome because of the intense element of emotional attachments so many of us have to our physical nature, and to those aspects of material existence which demand so much of our energy and attention. The possible loss of which awakens fear.

Survival is what is at stake for the vast, vast majority of our fellow beings. In that kind of intense situation the pursuit of spirituality and attending techniques for the transformation of consciousness would appear to be a luxury people involved in the desperate struggle for survival might think themselves well advised to avoid.

And avoid it many do, although many do not. Many ignore the inbred greed that materialistic philosophies encourage in materially-oriented beings for a simpler existence more in tune with the natural rhythms of the earth.

Health benefits from advanced medical discoveries aside, which people of lesser income may not be capable of enjoying, the advances of technological civilization promise far more than they can reasonably deliver.

And on closer examination, it appears clear that the levels of stress, anxiety and generally disturbing behavior rises considerably when we lose contact with the natural rhythms of the universe.

And as an unfortunate consequence, lose contact with our deep, inner selves to such an extent that we seem always to be swimming only on the surface level of the ocean of consciousness of which we are a part.

We may survive in such an unenlightened state, but we are not fully alive to the world, and know relatively little of ecstasy, rapture and bliss. The joy of existence has no rightful place in the world of rapid-fire technological progress and a corporate mentality focused only on the bottom line of maximum profitability.

The age of competition has its significant drawbacks, and it has nearly reached the end of the line in a world of rapidly-diminishing resources and environmental destruction on a massive scale.

Environmental destruction is not simply limited to the physical landscape; it also involves the elimination and extinction of many, many diverse and irreplaceable life forms on the planet by the bloodied, multi-colored hands of cruel, greedy and merciless human intervention and incessant attempts at domination and control for paper profit.

This, as well as the by-now traditional and habitual destruction of our fellow human beings upon the unsettled difference of an opinion. We may be the only species on the planet with warfare perpetually on our minds as an always inherent solution to our disagreements and disputes.

Not even the most savage beasts on the planet go about the constant and organized destruction of their competitors. Which may bring into question, considering our human history of open warfare and genetic forms of genocide, why it is that we call animals savage and human behavior civilized.

We can no longer justify the unjustifiable, but we nevertheless continue to avoid confronting serious issues as we tend to our little hearth fires and worry about the mortgage or the rent.

This is one of the unavoidable paradoxes, with often tragic consequences, of physical existence; the difficulty we face in reconciling the necessities of physical existence with our spiritual nature.

We are so caught up in the inevitable necessities of simply daily existence that most of us can ill-afford the luxury of looking at the big picture. For many of us, daily existence *is* the big picture.

And with good reason, for the big picture has become vague, cruel, heartless and distorted. The big picture is not a work of art, but a pale and emotionally-pallid kaleidoscope of portraits and attendant features all out of touch with each other, alienated from the fundamentals of peaceful and productive existence.

This may be the way things are, *and it is,* but it is not the way we want them to be. We may hope for change, or say we do, but if change threatens our comfort level and then actually appears coming head-long down the pike, it is all too often the thing with which we are most concerned, of which we are most afraid.

We seem to be drifting along towards a world we never made, but which we have carelessly allowed to come into existence. The forces of alienation and isolation have organized. They are powerful, but individually *we* are not.

It is *we* who are being organized by *them*, herded like cattle into our little play pens waiting for the final bell to ring that signals our turn at the slaughtering house. Urged along by punitive threats and the eager but intentionally misleading promptings of those who have sold their souls for thirty pieces of silver. And the opportunity to stand in the spotlight for their fifteen minutes of fame.

Those greedy few among us who live in luxury and relish power exist at the top levels of every human culture and society. They are energy vampires feeding at the trough of human suffering, skimming the choice cuts for themselves.

While it is characteristic of the plane of duality, so many of us, disempowered and afraid, are the very opposite of the power-elite. Zombies mindlessly going on about our business in the frantic search for succor and sustenance.

Cattle slowly and inevitably being led to the slaughter, unaware of what awaits them but restless as they intuitively sense something unpleasant is hidden in their immediate future. Does that feeling not strike a familiar note, a sense of impending doom and gloom that things are not right and perhaps never will be again. As though they ever were.

The Internet is filled with disgruntled voices of the masses that are fundamentally angry, no longer content to grumble in private, whose frustrations will not be content with private thoughts embraced in the loneliness of emotional and intellectual solitude instead of taking direct action in the company of like-minded souls.

The Internet has become a battlefield in which opposing armies of the night take up anonymous residence and begin hurling fusillade after fusillade of despair and discontent.

Meaningful or otherwise, the Internet is filled with critical and often harshly public ruminations, private thoughts for a public audience, something akin to a racial mind in turmoil.

And filled with multi-complexioned voices of criticism and complaint, speaking their truths as best they know them to anonymous persons and an eager and receptive audience the world over who have tuned in to the mind of humanity.

There is power in that, if it can be organized and directed for common purpose. How and by whom it will be directed is a matter that may soon be addressed, but most likely in a way the Internet was not created to serve. Entrenched forces of power and authority will inevitably attempt to censor the Internet by overt and heavy-handed legislative actions.

They will enact laws, ostensibly in the public interest although it is only private and corporate interests they are interested in defending, that will control the means and methods of Internet service and communication. It will be censorship, and it will be directed at controlling the flow of information and communication on a world-wide basis.

Or perhaps one unhappy day they will attempt to silence individual voices directly. Some day they may legislate that a computer chip must be installed in every computer that will allow central authorities to monitor its activities, and trace back to the point of origin any messages or Internet commentaries of which those authorities are suspicious.

In a time of international and domestic terrorism from any individual or organization that harbors fierce opinions, and lacks the control or morality to mediate them through means other than outright violence, this might seem like a good thing to some.

But to others, even when done in the name of national security and anti-terrorist protectionism it is nothing but fascism flying under the false flag of patriotism and self-protection. When people are silent as freedom dies, it dies not with a scream of agony but with a lonely whimper in the dark.

For those others it will be an excuse for the forces of power and authority, as Lord Acton prophesized, to become absolutely corrupted by absolute power to intrude on the activities of individual minds through the power of mass censorship.

Big brother will always rise to any occasion in which influence and power can be seized, and this certainly is one such possibility.

Unknown faces with grim intent, sitting in frozen silence in windowless cubicles, reading computer analyses of thoughts and ideas that threaten the total control over the minds of men that totalitarian forces may well be intent on achieving.

This does not offer us any hope of a happy future, unless we content ourselves with living in a world of computer matrixes, reality television that is anything but real, and news that is no longer news but carefully-crafted talking points that keep us in a state of pseudo-happiness, semi-content and mindlessly unaware of the world as it really is.

And so it became while we sat in silence in front of our entertainment devices as the world slowly slipped away from us, and we were left with nothing but our memories and our illusions. The matrix has come into being through human inaction and indifference, like a frog slowly boiling to death

So mindlessly unaware many of us may very well become without the means to communicate with like-minded souls. We will essentially be living in the stone age of information.

Our caves will be more comfortable and food will still be available but expensive. The air will still be breathable if one does not live too long as our lungs will tend to give out sooner than ever before because of pollution and radiation. But we will no longer be truly alive, we will have become zombies unaware that they are the walking dead.

True freedom will be only a distant memory, and liberty a myth that once we believed but have now been alerted, through the mass-infusion of talking points disguised as information, that liberty is and always was a threat to established good order.

More so now than ever because of the threat of terrorist activity, so that ultimately we are better off without it. New generations will never know the freedoms they are missing, the memory of which will have been reduced to a merely mythic past that never actually was. Memory is unreliable.

Thanks Be!, they will intone with reverence, for the safety and security of the rule of carefully-disguised martial law, under which we all may find ourselves living to which we will be obligated to swear fealty, our loyalty and allegiance. Like peasants on a medieval fiefdom, now become a state-sponsored reality.

Tenant-workers we may become, still living in a medieval landscape but with technological overtones. But peasants all the same while the rich and powerful live off the pickings and take the choice cuts for themselves.

Impossible though this all seems, we have been there many times before throughout our racial history. We tend to forget the past, just as there are those who have never studied the past and are unaware of the constant repetition of historical cycles in new and ever-improved forms.

Those who cannot remember the past are condemned to repeat it, a well-known historical maxim generally attributed to the philosopher George Santayana. Often quoted, always true.

There may very well have been vast periods of human history and human civilization of which we have been generally unaware and which are only now coming into the light of archeological analysis. Gone and forgotten, the lessons of their existence unremembered and unlearned.

But what we do know, which is still considerable, is that history tends to repeat itself as human civilizations run out of the energy that sustained them in their great periods of expansion and innovation.

But as always, where there is a period of expansion there always follows a period of contraction. It is the silent heartbeat of the cosmos, expansion and contraction, the yang and yin of existence, the great Tao.

And when that cycle of existence repeats, we fall back into survival modes as archetypes for sustained existence recycle and apply themselves to the rise and fall of civilizations.

The historical oversoul has seen it all, many times in many ways. We may well be heading now into a prolonged period of historical decline, with an attendant rise in fascism through whatever forms the impulse to fascist thinking and the urge to power comes into existence. Conservatism intends to preserve the past rather than embrace the future.

If we, as the collective force of humanity, cannot or will not learn from the realities of fascist histories we may inevitably succumb to that same force of existence. In this brave new world of technological genius and the potentially totalitarian impulses that always have and currently still do intend to control our thoughts and actions, we may not easily recover this time from what promises to be a disaster of epic-like proportions. World-wide control and domination by a handful of powerful and competing technologically-sophisticated cultural amalgamations and alliances.

Our minds and imaginations have been dulled by the force of social inertia. Stagnated by our various addictions to drugs, nicotine, alcohol, sex and social media outlets, we ignore our essential being by indulging in lesser satisfactions.

The Internet in particular, which allows us to pleasure ourselves through the fantasy fulfillment of our basest and most-easily fed lowest impulses. We postpone virtually nothing now that virtually anything we desire, in the virtual world of the Internet, is accessible in great and specific detail.

But all without the accompanying physical sensations which we were created to enjoy, and which make life both real, satisfying and pleasurable. And which, without the satisfaction of our most basic human needs and impulses, only adds to the stress and anxiety that is so deeply characteristic of modern existence in an increasingly cerebral but misguided culture.

Ease of access tends to dominate our thinking processes to the point that we make spontaneous choices without the virtue of hard and serious thinking about the worthiness of those choices. Along with the enormous freedom of information the Internet offers us comes the great responsibility of enlarging our mental aptitudes or contracting them through the power of our choices. But when we make our Internet choices, many of us do not choose well.

We want our freedoms, but many of us do not accept that freedom comes at a price. How we use it and what we use it for is a serious condition upon which freedom rests. Use it well and the rewards can be enormously gratifying. Misuse or abuse it and we suffer the consequences, which can be terrifying to the body, the mind and the spirit.

We are not necessarily dealing with natural and impersonal forces of existence when dealing with the sweep and sway of historical change. We are generally dealing with the minds of men who attempt, and succeed, in imposing their minds and personal will on the environment and the rest of us.

Benevolent officials may exist, but so do tyrants and fools who use power for selfish and immoral purposes. This seems so much a matter of chance that it is almost impossible to maintain good order in the affairs of men without superimposing some external authority on our free will.

To do so suggests that freedom and liberty are subject to compromise when they are not, but enforced compromise through external authority is not essentially suggestive of either freedom or liberty.

What is at stake when we do that is the submission of the formless into form, the imposition onto men's minds of some disciplined set of beliefs to which, deprived of the freedom of individual choice, we must all subscribe under penalty of law.

Reasonable or not, the will of the individual and the power of the many will be subject to the will of the empowered few, as represented by governing authorities. If this is the natural state of mankind, that we must always be ruled or over-ruled by some external authority to function in a meaningful way as a civilized force of existence. What does this suggest about the inherent ability of the human race to rule itself in a matured and productive manner?

Perhaps that is a function of racial maturity, and perhaps also the evidence suggests that as a race of sentient beings we are not yet there. Not yet ready to assume conscious control over our general evolution and collective well-being.

We may one day be on our way, but the exigencies of daily life today are so much in doubt for so many of us that we are virtually consumed by the absolute necessity to engage in the all-consuming business of sheer survival.

We have precious little free time to explore the nature of our existence, and often must rely on established traditions to find our rightful place in the universe. We take for granted what our traditions tell us, often questioning nothing for fear that we will raise more questions than those traditions can answer. Or that we can accept.

Some of us wear our spiritual blinders with relief that we do not have to see more than we can understand. And so we continue to stagnate without the possibility of fresh information or new ideas in our daily existence, even though that information and those ideas are freely available if we are willing to make the effort.

Some of us are, many of us are not. If we are not, nothing will change even if we do have the time, as so many of us now do, to explore our options and interact with others in meaningful and enlightening ways.

Perhaps there are those among us who are simply not ready for more advanced work along spiritual lines, or not yet ready to explore the nature of their own being and alternate ways of undergoing the human experience.

Perhaps also it is not a change of mind that is needed, but a change in consciousness itself. Changing our mind will not necessarily make it work any better, but accelerating our conscious evolution will.

What we may find, when we delve deeply into the inner workings of our psyche, is the bliss of being that radiates through the cosmos through the sheer presence of pure consciousness. And that induces a change in experience that can neither be denied nor forgotten, although acting on that change is a separate and distinct matter

Love, as we know it in all the various temporal human forms through which it makes its presence known, is the surface presence in all its diamante facets of the radiant bliss of our inner being.

Love is the truth of who and what we are, consciousness itself, and not simply the sentient biological forms through which it, and we, manifest on the material plane.

This is extraordinarily good news in this world of generally uninformed duality, in which good news is oft interred with the bad. Or so it would appear if we identify and experience ourselves only according to the surface appearance of things. Which is what most of us typically do, and which only a precious few, the spiritual adepts among us, do not.

A world in which love is not recognized, understood or experienced as the fundamental and ruling force of conscious existence is a world that is essentially inauthentic to its own true nature.

And that suggests that those who do not recognize the bliss of being as the fundamental nature of their inner self are forced to play out whatever role they may find that suits them. And thereby embrace whatever temporarily sustains their being, but which will not, of itself, fulfill them in accordance with genuine bliss.

We will not find ourselves in accord with our inner self and the infinite spirit of the universe as long as we identify ourselves only as game players in an inauthentic universe of our own making.

None of us are equal to the task of playing God, which is what we are essentially trying to do by creating our own rules for existence. We respond to the creation, but not necessarily the creator. And we empower the games we play, rather than the essential nature of our being along lines of spiritual authority and harmony.

We cannot fool ourselves for long into believing that by following artificial rules of existence we will find our bliss. We will not. True bliss is not something that can be created by human hands and minds within the limitations of the space/time continuum.

If we imagine we can create something always and absolutely authentic to its own nature through artificial means, we will soon realize that we cannot use inauthentic methods to begin the process and achieve success.

Anything that is created is always subject to eventual change, and that can never lead to the absolute integrity of immortal being on this plane of duality. True bliss can never be subject to chance, change or the misfortunes of accidental occurrences.

In human terms, true bliss comes through self-realization, the experience of absolute and complete oneness of being. And that can only be found when we are in complete communion with the source of being itself. When we are one with ourselves, and consequently the divine spirit that resides within our being.

Such a profoundly empowering and fulfilling destiny lies within the vanguard of human affairs if we are willing to put aside, or forced to put aside through learned experience, the distractions of careless living that consume our energy and attention, and blind us to the truth of our existence.

It is no longer possible, without facing the disastrous effects of corrupt leadership and totalitarian energies, to avoid a truthful encounter with the questions of existence that put so harsh a strain on our conscious-awareness and conscience when we go to such absurd attempts to avoid them.

We buy into foolish attempts to ritualize our existence that offer us salvation through assumptions without any direct evidence that supports the conclusions we are force-fed and intimidated to accept. Both religion and science do this, each in their own way.

Religion asks us to accept on faith what cannot be proven, and then makes a doctrine out of faith. A doctrine in which many people have no faith, but which they are told is essential to their spiritual health and well-being.

A doctrine which is without essential meaning considering that the founders of those religions, or so we are to believe, acted out of their own direct experiences rather than from the theological assumptions of other men.

If we object to these manifold assumptions masquerading as divine revelation we are informed that the founding figures were divine or nearly so, perfected in some manner which we are unable to understand or achieve ourselves.

And consequently their teachings, or the teachings ascribed to them by latter followers or historically unknown persons, may not be questioned on pain of heresy or death.

A convenient doctrine if one does not wish to answer questions which are unanswerable, but not particularly useful if our intention is to find truth rather than doctrinal submission.

Science asserts that its doctrines must be supported by evidence, and this is largely so as the history of real science demonstrates. But the premise of the Big Bang theory makes a fundamental assertion that is more in the nature of an assumption, and an article of faith, than a statement of fact.

The Big Bang theory claims that the universe exploded into existence, and that everything that occurred since then can be explained by scientific theory. Perhaps so, but then again, what was the cause of that initial explosion? And in what unknown source did all the fundamental energies of the physical universe of which we are now aware have their original, *dare we say it,* creation?

Some scientists may insist that the question of meaning has no place in science, which is only concerned with factual evidence. But this is to ignore the possibility, as well as belief, that the concept of meaning draws forth a reciprocating response from the universe which may through unknown ways further the pursuit and acquisition of knowledge.

Meaning and purpose may be an inherent factor within the potentially unknown and unexamined make-up of universal energies. And may call some thing or quality into existence that fulfills an inherent necessity for purpose and fulfillment. And in doing so, in fulfilling the purposeful activities of energetic being and interaction, directs the manifest affairs of the cosmos.

Order rather than chaos may be an inherent, inborn factor within the unmanifest and manifest energies of the universe. Both states of being and non-being may co-exist simultaneously, order as a state of directed fulfillment and chaos a state of incomplete, inchoate manifestation of an original impulse towards being.

Evolution, the plain fact that we are here, strongly implies that order can and does come from an inchoate state of unmanifest and manifest energy. That evolution is an ongoing activity in creation, and conversely, that some evolving forms of material being will stagnate and die out if an evolutionary impasse is reached.

All created forms can still evolve and change, no matter how satisfactory a state of being may have been reached. But for a species to continue to thrive it must be able to continually adapt to change and benefit from the result.

Changing circumstances require reciprocating responses from the subject under scrutiny, or the survival of an individual, or a civilization will be in jeopardy. Species suffer extinction when they cannot find the means to overcome a challenge that threatens their continued existence. This is not news, but it *is* true and it *is* the reality in which we exist.

On the plane of duality life must be aware and capable of responding to change lest changing circumstances overtake individual or collective existence. A species is doomed to failure if it cannot recognize and adapt to whatever existence brings forth. Nothing is guaranteed except change.

The universe might be an enormous teaching device in the nearly-infinite university that is the cosmos. The processes of duality might be a way in which spirit enlightens the discrete forms of consciousness that arise through the evolutionary process, beginning, if not continuing, the education of the individual soul and enhancing the spirit.

Duality is clearly an enormous challenge to the continuous existence of conscious, self-aware existence, the arena in which life is forced to learn and grow, expand or perish. Neither option at the hands of an indifferent fate, but because a particular life form was or was not capable of further mobility and upward growth on the evolutionary scale of being.

We might not wish to think of ourselves in this somewhat reductionist manner, but it may be that life is an experiment in being. Nothing is guaranteed us, and just as the Neanderthals went either extinct or into hiding, so might we.

Not at the hands of an indifferent God, but at the hands of the indifferent masses of humanity who coasted along without taking conscious charge of their destiny. And who left their fate in the greedy hands of the empowered few, whose only regard was for themselves.

No price is too high for our survival, and no religious tradition can guarantee our survival. Neither rites, nor rituals, nor ceremonies of spiritual incantations can guarantee us success in our human pursuits and earthly endeavors. They may have a calming influence, but when dawn comes it is always back to business as usual.

Nor can any high-minded magical formulations guarantee that we will survive our own evolution. It might very well be that the best they can do is provide guidance and spiritual instruction for the education of our soul, and that is no small achievement considering the spiritual sloth that has overtaken our species.

But fundamentalism in all its essential elements clearly does not and cannot represent spiritual evolution in any regard. It is simply the ego's descent into a spiritual underground of its own making, filled with chains, emoluments and illusions.

Fundamentalism tends to function as a reactionary retreat into a world that never was, never could be and never will be except in the pseudo-mythical imaginations of displaced religious refugees into their private versions of a dark and dismal Disneyland for the spirit.

Left unmonitored and unregulated, fundamentalism can become a violent reaction to the spontaneous activities of evolutionary change, and as such prohibits the free range of spirit in exploring the potentials of human existence.

What would life be like without the ability to choose, along with a variety of choices available for the continuing education of our soul? We would not be alive in the fullest sense of the word; we would be living an existence of enforced spiritual slavery not necessarily or at all of our own choosing.

That could not possibly be a useful condition in which to live a fulfilling existence. There could be no forward momentum in such a situation. Without the impulse for growth and maturation our evolutionary momentum would stagnate and suffocate of its own weight. We would eventually be slated for extinction.

We must grow and mature, and inevitably plumb the inner depth chambers of our being. The answers we seek to the mysteries of existence, of our own being, can only be found within our own psyche. We must learn to turn inward.

That and that alone, is the truest and most useful purpose of any religion. Neither high-minded bigotry through the denial of other paths to the divine, nor the misuse of spiritual teachings to aggrandize the few at the expense of the many will aid us in our spiritual endeavors.

And certainly not meant to bind us mindlessly fast to relatively primitive interpretations of any ancient religious belief system, enforced through the current organization of religious traditions in institutional forms. Religion is not the enemy, but when it denies the mystical path it poaches away at our freedoms through negligence and repression.

Institutions in any form are not generally conducive to the free-flow of ideas or the free activities of spirit. Freedom is all too often perceived by institutional authorities as a threat to institutional control.

Freedom is a necessity for the individual, but it is treated as a luxury by institutional authorities when their unhampered freedom to rule over the rest of us is challenged.

Religion should take us beyond those political distinctions masquerading as religious requirements, however they are disguised or dressed up for the occasion. True religious activities should be focused on freeing us from bondage to material forms and the enchaining ego-structures of the mind. And only towards the direct knowledge of universal spirit as it manifests through corporal forms.

This also is evolution in action. This is the way we consciously progress and move into the enlightenment of full consciousness. It frightens some of us to such an overt extent that we prefer to remain in spiritual darkness rather than enter the light chambers of the soul.

So attached are we to our material forms and the possibilities that haunt our future plans that our present existence is predicated only on fulfilling our impossible hopes for the future in the present form of our incarnation.

That our incarnation in whatever form we currently occupy will one day end is not something very many of us are willing to entertain as a philosophical, religious and psychological necessity. Or that we should be thinking along these lines of nature as a necessary condition of our continued long-term health and well-being. Of existence itself.

But it is. How we prepare for the ending of this limited human existence is as necessarily important to us as how we have lived it. The means may not necessarily justify the end, but what happens when life reaches the ending stages should influence the manner in which we have lived, and the contributions we made that have justified our existence.

We are taught by our spiritual elder brothers and sisters that life is an incredible gift, and that it should be lived according to the guidelines of spirit. But we act in a sometimes contrary fashion, as though it is we who were the creators, and subject to none but our own authority.

And this is something we will have to unlearn as a species if we are to survive our own evolution. What qualities of learned and earned wisdom do we have in our arsenal of resources that assure us we will continue on as an evolving species?

So far we have demonstrated neither the emotional maturity and social skills, nor any inherent forms of spiritual wisdom to manage the creation only according to our own terms of endearment. We cannot even successfully manage our own affairs in our petty little fiefdoms.

We might not be a very good prospect for long-term survival considering that we cannot manage even a decade or so without constantly resorting to warfare as a deadly means of creating conflict or settling disputes with each other.

Do any of us honestly believe that as a race of beings we have demonstrated the wisdom and knowledge to manage our evolution only according to our present state of being? Could anyone defend any such absurd belief?

Where do we go for help in a world in which there does not appear to be a last and final resource for fair and impartial justice. In our present state of being we are essentially thrown back on our own resources.

The question that should be haunting our minds and consciousness is how far we have gone in exploring the inner reaches of our psyche.

Is there some state of conscious existence within us in which negativity in any form simply does not and cannot exist. A state of unified wholeness and integral being that puts us in accord with all others who have reached that same inner state of unmotivated bliss.

Yes, we are assured by spiritual masters. *No,* we are informed by those for whom skepticism and despair are the natural order of existence, and will do nothing to mitigate the terms of their surrender to existential despair.

Those who have no answer are stuck in the essential problem of duality. They can move neither to the left nor to the right. Neither affirm nor deny the truths or untruths of any or either position. The case for spirituality is as empty of specific content for them as is the case for chaos and meaningless.

In essence they suffer from a premature paralysis of the will, the inability to act in any cause or direction that might succeed in earning them a safe and secure sinecure in spite of the religious and philosophical confusion that is a marked characteristic of our times.

They are in spiritual disarray, disjointed and discouraged, and they regard that state of malaise as the natural order of things. They cannot think outside the box because they do not know they are in a box.

They regard the limits of their imaginations as the limitless state of the universe. More and only more of the same with no possibility of parole, and no regard for the ultimate effects of entropy.

Unaware that their continued state of unknowing, like the universe itself, is fated eventually to run down. They suffer from lethargy, which can make them indifferent to their fate.

Lethargy in this regard can and does lead to spiritual sloth, well-known as one of the seven deadly sins. Wrath, anger, sloth, pride, lechery, envy and gluttony. Spiritual sloth is deadly because it often leads to a premature denial of the true nature of our existence, and even suicide of the will.

We are spiritual beings living in an immense universe created by an unknown but nevertheless magnificent and unfathomable creative force of unimaginable intelligence that brings order to its creation, the cosmos.

Spiritual sloth closes the door to that essential experience of inner enlightenment. It denies us both the energy and enthusiasm to begin the investigation of our inner nature, and leaves us without the essential inner resources to find our true self within the immensity of a strange and often hostile environment.

We are left on our own, ostensibly alone with no apparent possibility of finding our way out of the intellectual and emotional maze that our confusions about existence have engendered. Wisdom cannot flourish in such a barren environment, nor can enlightened progress be made in ways that further our evolution and affirm our rightful and inherent place in the cosmos.

We have nowhere else to look for the solution to our spiritual dilemmas but within our own being. The cycle of spiritual entropy in which we are immersed has led us, deaf and dumb, down a blind alley after centuries of abuse and neglect. And the truth is, we all know it. We are aware, and our awareness cannot be ignored, neither hidden nor denied.

We are in spiritual disarray because our essential institutions have failed to lead us beyond their continued insistence that they, each of them and all of them in their own ways, have the one and only revealed truth. But inevitably leading nowhere other than a downward spiral.

And it is they, each one and every one of them, who say the same thing over and over. They and they alone are in sole possession of the keys to the kingdom. But imagine believing any such thing when the kingdom includes the cosmos and all that is in it. That mankind should be capable of uttering any such nonsense is arrogant foolishness of the highest order.

Without their institutional guidance and moral support, or so they maintain, we are all doomed to a relatively inert existence of religious ignorance. Even though, as we all now publically recognize, there may be some larger questions about the ability of institutional morality to enforce for itself and its adherents the rules by which it insists the rest of us should live and must abide.

Not because they are heartless and cruel, but because they insist on substituting archaic principles and meaningless mythically-derived rules of order for the inner experiences of spiritual enlightenment. Which is what they should be teaching, but do not because they cannot.

They cannot teach what they do not know, what they have not realized and achieved for themselves, the knowledge of the depths of their own inner being. And the direct inner experience of God-realization and the true state of spiritual awakening.

This may be because they deny the experience either actually exists, or can be achieved by anyone other than the founding figures whose teachings they follow. And fearful, perhaps, that to abandon the disciplined approach that an institution requires to disseminate its teachings might be replaced by and suffer from the chaos and disorder of individual experience in conflict with institutional discipline.

And that is the risk that enlightened spirituality represents for unenlightened institutional thinking. Not that that is always the case, but enough so that, of itself, institutional thinking represents a repressive force of immense power.

It might be one causal factor that holds us all back from seeking an enlightened experience of existence and knowledge of our own being. It might be the illness for which it pretends to be the cure.

Experience is the best teacher, but without that essential experience of inner knowing we are lost among the stars, adrift in a universe in which duality is the apparently prevailing order of existence. And nothing beside remains.

We have a choice. We can accept this view of existence and continue living in the mental fog that spiritual sloth induces in even the best and brightest among us. Or we can take a stand and begin to look deeply into matters we have traditionally been encouraged to avoid, or which we have allowed others to decide for us. The choice is always ours.

Four

The choice is always ours

One of the responsibilities that comes with freedom, and there are many, is the requirement that we make as honest and complete an effort as possible to look into our beliefs deeply and with absolute integrity.

We ought to be questioning the sources of our beliefs, taking nothing for granted and accepting nothing on faith alone. Especially so since faith, which can be a noble concept in the proper circumstance, and often a necessary tool when we are in search of additional evidence to support a theory or an as yet unproven idea, is itself neither proof nor evidence.

But there should be a proper context in which we rely on faith, for without a reasonable framework we may simply be indulging in magical thinking and these are not magical times. The magic lies in the research techniques and results, not the fantasy wish-fulfillment scenario which some of us substitute for the hard and difficult task of researching our subject.

Religion often relies on the need for faith to justify its claims to belief, but when it does that it is making its case in violation of standard rules of evidence. There is no available evidence when faith is invoked in a religious belief system.

Clearly, the rules of evidence that apply in science or legal affairs are not presented in the same manner or judged according to the same rules of evidence that the religious scenario admits before the spiritual bar for judgment. And which we are not encouraged, or allowed, to question or judge for ourselves.

This is not good for business in the long run, and might be one of the reasons that organized religion is losing a great deal of its appeal according to contemporary standards and beliefs.

We are being asked to submit our spiritual health and well-being to a religious system of belief that can prove none of its claims, but yet insists that it is so flawless that beyond its institutional judgments and hierarchical traditions there is neither appeal nor salvation.

Not an especially helpful attitude in this age of information, particularly in the age of the Internet in which nearly all things are possible. Information can be sought out and accessed no matter what prohibitions assorted members of religious institutions legislate through formal doctrines or theological interpretations presented as dogma.

Anyone can find out almost anything anonymously, under cover of a user name so that the true identity of even the most casual inquiry will remain a secret between that person and his conscience.

The problem lies not in the availability of information, the problem lies in the willingness of the individual to devote any portion of his, or her, time and energy towards looking into matters of the spirit and the soul.

Is such an activity any less important than an evening intoxicated with whatever form of intoxication of choice one prefers. An evening absorbed by cable programming and the willful and willing suspension of disbelief in the pursuit of entertainment.

Or watching an organized group of adult men throwing, hitting or generally battering a small rubber object and each other in organized mayhem for a prolonged period of time.

Or driving very loud, fast and dangerous sport vehicles in endless circles along and around a common track until a prescribed number of cycles is completed by one contestant sooner than the competing others.

These are not truly functionally-conscious choices, they are simply socially approved addictions to speed and semi-controlled danger. And whatever victory is claimed adds precious little to the ongoing activities of our general efforts in any serious regard or endeavor.

Not that it is wrong in any sense to watch or participate in these kind of leisure activities, only that the amount of energy, time and resources spent in pursuing them is simply not justified by the results.

We want to be amused in life, which is fine. We want relief from the daily anxieties of life, which is also fine, and we even want relief from the Sturm und Drang of exalting nature, feeling, and human individualism.

But almost anything and everything carried out to the extreme arc of its existential swing presents us with the nearly intolerable burden of asking serious questions and anticipating serious answers but with little response.

And then scrutinizing whatever answers appear closely when whatever results manifest and unexpectedly prove to be a worrisome burden.

Our ability to absorb or entertain highly questionable notions is limited by our willingness to tolerate nonsense. Especially so when it involves highly questionable religious dogma burdened by the lack of supporting evidence for its conclusions.

Many of us may have an automatic default position to fall back on when this occurs, which may also be why so many of us pass up any opportunity or occasion to begin the serious investigation of what we believe and why we believe it.

In an unexamined life faith might simply be a standard default position in the face of opposition, rather than the occasion for the opening of the spiritual heart in its embrace of the cosmos and all that entails in the ordering of a life trajectory.

A characteristically unconscious response to the paralysis of the will occasioned by the harshly conflicting encounter between subtle if not overt mystical aspirations and the rational exegesis of logical analysis.

Often disguised within the stereotypical and conventional call and response traditions that takes themselves to be the reality for which they are only a diffident rider on a pale horse.

We must learn not only to challenge what we imagine reality to be, but our interpretations of what that might actually mean. Worse than evidence being tampered with is the frail and faulty logic we empower in the vain and futile attempt to justify conclusions that have already been reached without the benefit of counsel.

The complaining person at the bar is humanity itself, the spirit of man that seeks truth rather than doctrinal suppositions masquerading as honest inquiry. There is nothing honest about reaching a conclusion about serious and substantial issues without first completely examining the evidence that comes down on all sides of the issue.

And then judging according to the weight of real and factual evidence, as opposed to the subjective weight we bring to bear on any issue with which we are emotionally entangled. This allows prejudice to exert a powerful influence on what should rightly be an objective, impersonal and honest evaluation.

This tends to happen when emotions run high and personal preferences are allowed to interfere in supposedly objective editorial processes. Some of us prefer to judge the world only according to our personal preferences, rather than according to what the world may actually be on its own terms.

But experience teaches us, or ought to, that the world will not conform to our demands or expectations. It is we who will have to adapt to the world, not by subjecting our preferences to the will of others, but by recognizing the nature of reality and learning to live within it to our maximum benefit.

And in this regard, the beliefs, experiences and traditions of others may help us navigate our path through the confusions and complexities of the world. But in truth, we will all have to find our own way, in our own time and for our own purposes through the entangled filaments of material reality.

The beliefs, experiences and traditions of others may help, but we must all learn to walk our own walk, and speak the truth as best we know it with no or little regard for social conventions, religious pressures or political consequences.

An inevitably difficult task when faced with the various ways in which we are encouraged, if not forced, to conform to whatever voices speak with the agreement of general consensus. Or which speak with the authority of power, through any form in which power manifests.

A solemn act of personal empowerment when we make the sincere and determined effort to find our own authentic voice. Something not to be undertaken lightly or prematurely when social rejection is almost automatically expectable.

When one rides alone through the forest, without the security of companions and consensus in search of the Grail Castle and the Holy Grail, the journey will be fraught with danger and the loss of social approbation.

The call to spirit does not insure that we will have an easy time of it. On the contrary, we may expect the very opposite, that when we are called to find the truth of our existence we will face opposition of every sort, in every way imaginable. And that we should not expect to win every battle.

Invisible hands may reach out to us, and we may find ourselves the beneficiaries of material bounty, useful advice and here and there a bit of praise for our efforts. But we should also expect that as in all things of this world, we can expect to suffer.

Spirituality is not an escape from the inevitable processes of aging and dying, or from suffering in all the manifold ways in which we humans suffer. But spirituality does offer a way to live in the world that in a sense transcends suffering.

What undergoes suffering is the individual ego-mind and physical body. But as we actually are in spirit-consciousness, we are neither. We are the observing consciousness within, the witness-observer with which we ought to identify ourselves.

This is not an idea, a concept or a belief system. It is an experience of the highest order, the experience of one's inner identity as a spiritual entity undergoing a physical experience. This inner recognition is the highest and most solemn purpose of any spiritual undertaking.

The consequence of which, when solemnly undertaken, may often lead to social alienation and religious isolation, if not actual persecution. There is always a price to be paid for the process of individuation and the resulting singularity of individual identity.

If we expect that spirituality will free us from social expectations and any attending pressures, be aware that society will always find a way to make its presence known and its power and influence felt.

Nothing so threatens the collective voice of social approbation and authority but that its messages and demands of self-enforced conformity go unmet, either ignored or rejected. It is a violent incursion on conformity, and will not be tolerated by those of little faith.

And that is essentially how the path of spiritual freedom and the enlightenment of individual consciousness threatens social and religious establishments. What is involved is conformity to a centralized force of will, but what is at stake is the freedom of the individual to be himself or herself to the absolute and utmost degree. With only the self-discovered and self-empowered authenticity of individual being and experience to give voice to the integrity of one's being.

The rise of consciousness most significantly involves the education of the spirit. The necessary conditions of worldly education and personal empowerment are somewhat secondary in that regard, critical though they are in materialistic terms.

Other than for purposes of absolute and immediate survival, along with the necessity for the fulfillment of our earthly trajectories, we are here for the education of our spirit and the fulfillment of our soul's purpose. What that may be is a necessary object of the spiritual search many of us are actively involved in undertaking.

What is of prime importance to our evolutionary survival is that we find and understand from within our individual psyche the true condition of our existence. And the spiritual nature of our being, which some of us tend to avoid by masking our real needs under the guise of spiritual materialism.

Techniques for the exploration of the inward-bound nature of our existence are necessary adjuncts in the search for meaning and purpose. What we do and how we do it in this regard may be problematical for many of us who are deeply immersed in a materialistic environment, with seemingly few if any opportunities to expand the search or even undertake the journey.

This is the point at which we have stagnated when so many of us have given over our spiritual health and well-being for the standard conventions of ritualistic responses and formulaic incantations that lead only to a state of pseudo-spiritual but essentially inert sentimentality.

This attitude of spiritual torpor not only leads to stagnation, but to various degrees of frustration and despair. When our spiritual imagination is cut off from its source we are left behind with only our own individual emotional resources to fall back on.

Ultimately, they avail us nothing. Spirituality is not focused on sentimentality or incantations of high emotional-regard, it is the experience of higher dimensions of being and the transformation of consciousness to achieve that end.

Confusion is the inevitable result of spiritual isolation. And then comes the feeling of alienation when we have nothing in which to believe outside ourselves except whatever good fortune comes our way. And then follows despair when our good fortune has run its course.

And whatever else we have managed to accumulate during the course of our lives that offers us comfort and security, however unsecured that might be for lack of a fundamental accord with the universe. Inevitably when the end comes, there is nothing left but a few dried crumbs and the picked over coldly served-forth left-overs when the feast is over.

If we have nothing other than the private world in which we live to sustain us it will become nearly impossible to relate to each other in meaningful ways unless we make the determined effort to do so. Even so, our best efforts may well deteriorate when our strength and goodwill fail us in times of unexpected stress and needless anxiety.

We need something of lasting significance to believe in, and for many of us this is because of an inherent sense that as we are today, we exist in an existential environment of our own making in which we have been cut off from the primal source of being. And have nothing left except our pale philosophies to sustain us in life.

It simply does not matter how hard or in how many ways we try to resuscitate the past to address this issue when the energy that had sustained former endeavors runs down and dissipates in the closed energy system of religious certitude and closure. The religious assurances that once were ours when we were children have gone forever. The past can neither be resuscitated nor revived.

One way or another, we must find our way back to unity and wholeness before we run amok and destroy ourselves and our environment. But we cannot do that by turning the chronological clock of historical epochs backwards, and recreating through spiritual time-travel the beliefs of past cultures.

Those now discarded beliefs were originally created for a people long since gone from daily life and activities. Time marches on, and so does human knowledge. Any such attempts to live according to past beliefs quickly disintegrate under the critical scrutiny of current knowledge. And can exist, if at all, only in the fevered imaginations of fundamentalist zealots.

The problem of spirituality and a spiritual belief system in which to believe remains behind as each age slips into history. Every age must face this on its own terms. But the energy of the proposed solutions prior cultures have created and believed in will usually vanish along with the people who proposed them within generations. As, most likely, will ours when we too have vanished from the scene and the frontier of human knowledge moves on and advances our fundamental interests in newer lines of thought.

Increased knowledge of material reality and the human condition always adds to our understanding of the universe. An understanding comes into generally-accepted acclamation that the prior knowledge, the wisdom in which former cultures believed, was, after all, only assumptions misunderstood and taken for factual evidence.

The more we learn the more we must adapt our belief systems beyond the sentimental attachments which defined our prior attachments. Our spiritual inheritance is enormous, if we take into account the whole of mankind's efforts to reach the spiritual star that shines within.

But if we rely on the past as our spiritual guide for the future we will come up short. And we will suffer for the consequences. We must find our way home to the inner source of guidance and nurture, and we must begin by first accepting that there is a spiritual reality that dwarfs our own pale efforts.

Disbelief and denial take enormous tolls on our health and well-being, and will continue to do so with mounting disarray and disadvantage the longer we postpone the inevitable day of reckoning.

Age brings us closer to this realization than the relative immaturity and ignorance of youth, and then the accommodations as well that middle age forces us to make in the inevitable pursuit of material comfort and security.

Age alone teaches us the illusory nature of all physical stages of human growth and maturity when we have passed the period of striving and can look back in sorrow and relief. And the fleeting nature of all we pursue in the matter of earthly goals becomes ever that much more clear.

They vanish in an instant, the dreams of youth and the achievements of a lifetime of struggle and achievement, like phantoms in a dark and eternal night of nothingness. We are guaranteed nothing, which time demonstrates to even the most determined among us. Ultimately, our best efforts will vanish with the morning mists and the morning star.

In a spiritual context they are useless in terms of lasting security and self-knowledge. Everything that exists is subject to the vicissitudes that time always brings to any earthly endeavor, even our own physical existence.

If we truly care about the issue of our spiritual being we will have to make the serious effort to experience that inner reality for ourselves. There is no other way. We have to begin to change our approach and turn our minds towards investigating the interior landscape of our psyche.

And believe this: that something much greater than our individual being exists that brings order and meaning to our lives. We must above all accept the reality of the spiritual dimension. And in that direction we will find ourselves, and the truest meaning of our existence.

This is something that Hamlet finally learns after he has exhausted his own efforts to fulfill the conditions of his problematical existence. And then experiences first-hand the influence of the spiritual realm in his life. It is neither dogma nor theology that influences his life-changing affirmation. He is convinced by experience, his own experience but not the sayings or doings of others.

The spiritual realm has appeared in his life and provided him with the proof that theology and philosophy could not offer. Experience is always the best teacher in any situation, and it is experience that we are after ourselves, not religious dogma or philosophical speculation.

Hamlet explains his change of mind to his friend Horatio, and the spiritual enlightenment he is resolved to follow. *There's a special providence in the fall of a sparrow. If it be now, 'tis not to come. If it be not to come, it will be now. If it be not now, yet it will come—the readiness is all. Since no man of aught he leaves knows, what is 't to leave betimes? Let be.*

The readiness is all? Readiness for what? The readiness to accept life for what it is. To accept whatever come our way, and to rest assured that whatever does come our way is for us to deal with in the best way we can, with whatever is at hand, with the firm and certain belief that our life is securely in the hands of the Creator.

There is a special providence, a divine hand that guides the affairs of even a fallen sparrow. Which is what we are, fallen sparrows all. The spiritual quandary he was in when the adventure began is summarized when he questions existence itself. *To be or not to be,* he wonders, whether being alive is even worth the struggle to reconcile the seemingly impossible dilemmas that life has presented him with.

When Hamlet arrives at the realization of the spiritual nature of reality, that there is, in fact, a guiding hand in the creation of divine origin, that question no longer has meaning for him.

He answers the famously-resounding question of his earlier soliloquy himself when he says to Horatio, *Let be!* We must shout out a resounding *Yes!* to the universe, and live with gratitude for the experience of life whatever comes our way.

According to the spiritually-oriented philosophical position that Hamlet finally reaches, what is it to fear death, why bother with trifles, when there is a divine hand at work in the universe.

What will be, will be, he reasons, and for reasons of which we might not always be aware, but in His Hands we should place our trust. Hamlet believes this because he has had experiences that lead to this inescapable conclusion for him, and for no earthly reason or rational belief that would satisfy others not of a similar disposition.

All shall be well, and all shall be well, and all manner of things shall be well, wrote Dame Julien of Norwich. The experiences Hamlet has had, which he has interpreted along spiritual lines of reasoning and belief, are reason enough for him to believe in an ultimate spiritual reality. He has had his own experiences which led him to this position, let others have their own. And we ours as well.

All earthly endeavors, along with all familiar modes of reasoning and conventional belief offered neither the proof nor the closure that the certitude of earned experience brings. Hamlet has had powerful experiences, certain now of his spiritual ground, and acting from a newly-formed central core of belief and psychological stability.

And so should we all seek our own experiences of spiritual integrity and well-being. And so can we all, if we will turn our inner attention towards the source of being with an open mind and an eager heart. Sincerity and openness should guide our affairs, not philosophical determinism or religious hypocrisy masquerading as revelation.

Or on the other side of duality, the despair of free-wheeling nihilistic delusions that strip us of our spiritual conscience, relegating our moral concerns to the gray area between hope and despair, freedom and servitude, free will and the spiritual obligations of the creation towards the creative source.

We will make significant progress in transcending duality when we seek out and understand the inner experiences that define our being. And then begin the exploration of alternate states of consciousness, rather than simply accept the traditional role as recipients of conventionally-transmitted knowledge.

This avails us precious little when it comes to achieving an enlightened state of being. Knowledge is not synonymous with wisdom. It should be clear by now that the enlightenment of the individual soul concerning the reality of spirit is the goal of evolution. Nothing less will do.

We can no longer endorse the pseudo-spiritual medieval caste system that conventional religious concepts teach. Spiritual servitude is not the relationship we should assume exists between humanity and the divine force within existence, the true source of all that is.

We are part of that divine force of creation, far more than simply indentured earthly servants of an inadequately defined spiritual overlord. And we absolutely must begin to think in more sophisticated terms than any tradition that teaches us to be afraid of the divine instead of enjoying a reciprocally-loving relationship.

We are concerned now with the nature of existence, and especially the role of the divine in human affairs. We should take this seriously, and avoid the archetypal tendency to think in terms of fear instead of love. When we do that we will have prematurely judged reality according to incomplete evidence, and an only partial and extremely limited understanding of the terms of our existence.

Generation after generation comes and goes, all attempting to close the books on reality, each formulating theory after theory about the nature of existence and the meaning behind it all. Forgetful that theories alone can never take the place of experience.

There is no intellectual, sentimental or emotionally-based theory that can substitute for the direct experience of mystical revelation. Nothing we are taught can ever prepare us for the shock of recognition, to borrow Melville's famous phrase, when we have a direct encounter with the divine.

How that can happen is not subject to analysis or scrutiny for its message to be known. That it happens is the issue, not any analytic attempt to descriptively categorize the means or methods of the divine. If we dismiss the mystical experience because we do not understand it we miss the point and the adventure. The Pequod will have sailed without us.

We cannot hold on to the infinite in order to take it apart to describe its workings. The experience of divine encounter is not subject to laboratory analysis or scientific investigation.

The truth that results from the experience is what matters, nothing else. The tail does not wag the dog.

If we imagine that we can somehow control the creative intelligence that has fashioned the universe through logical analysis, intellectual objectivity or laboratory experimentation we are foredoomed to failure.

We do that because we seek proof, and will not believe in infinite spirit without material evidence. We want to judge the divine according to the same means and methods that we judge material reality. But when we do that we gain nothing, only diminishing the opportunity to find an inner accord with a greater existence. Can the part ever know the whole?

Do we need to measure the distance from the Earth to the Sun in order to see the Sun. Does anyone really believe that the intelligence that rules the cosmos can be analyzed and understood by such relative newcomers to the creation as the human race. Are we not simply deluding ourselves when we make judgments about the source of life based only on our own subjective suppositions.

The proof we seek will most probably never be found in mathematical formulae, laboratory experiments, dogmatic theorizing or re-creating ancient rites and rituals of re-enactment. The proof we seek can only come through direct experience, when we have put ourselves in accord with the divine. Who has ever satisfied their hunger by looking at a picture of a gourmet meal?

A greater glory awaits us than the simplistic reductionalist thinking of material rationalists and philosophical materialism disguised as reality, passing its precipitate conclusions off as evidence. Or the concrete rituals that formal religious enthusiasts substitute for the mystical experience, which they themselves have never had and likely never will.

Beliefs are not evidence, and are all too often supported by nothing more substantial than subjective opinions dressed up in entertaining but potentially misleading ways. The question for those who maintain that there is nothing after death is: *How would they know?* What is their evidence and by what method did they arrive at their conclusions.

The subject deserves far more serious attention along the lines of consciousness research than mere subjective opinionating relying on inadequate research, and premature conclusions based on materialistic neo-Darwinian models that assume total understanding of the processes of life, death and whatever next may come.

There is an implied assumption in that kind of speculative philosophizing that we are material beings only, and nothing more than that. Merely sentient, self-aware protoplasmic carbon-based life forms with a limited life span and doomed to individual extinction.

And what is the proof for that as well, other than the evidence that comes only from our physical senses. Our mystical traditions and the experiences that come when our psychic senses are energized inform us that a different order of reality exists than can be accessed only through a transformed consciousness.

This is clearly a challenge to our standard but supposedly undeveloped experience of reality. And should it not be investigated by serious researchers, not polemicists with an adversarial disposition.

Yes, of course it should. We have barely begun exploring our world and the cosmos. The exploitation of our environment and natural resources is not in the same category of knowledge and experience as the exploration of the nature of things. And especially not their relation to the whole of existence. In that we are merely beginners.

So let us begin to rethink our assumptions about human life, consciousness and the intelligence of the universe. Clearly the human body has an intelligence of its own that has no need of our conscious control. The body knows what to do and how to do it, while we have only the vaguest knowledge, if at all, of how our body works when we are in it.

Like passengers in the human vehicle of manifestation, we are subject to the episodic nature of the ride but inadequately prepared to partake of the multi-dimensional and perhaps even multi-sensory aspects of the journey.

Which lies in the exploration and transformation of consciousness, not simply the accumulation of material wealth, pretty toys that enchant us and come in many sizes and shapes, or booty collected from our various enterprises.

Caught up in these endeavors we become little more than enthusiastic collectors of whatever suits our fancy. But when the experience of physical embodiment is over we take nothing with us that will advance our evolutionary interests as the disembodied conscious entities we are in our soul essence.

We should enjoy the human journey, certainly, but there is far more to the earthly adventure that simply the excitement of physical experience and the accumulation of material goods. Beyond all that there is God.

Many of us have lost a sense of the sacred, a connection to the infinite and creative intelligence of the universe. Instead, we have been force-fed a steady diet of institutional rules and religious regulations. With hypocrisy dancing in attendance and masquerading as religious fervor.

But generally speaking, most of these are little more than ineffective rites and meaningless rituals that offer nothing of transcendent value, except the unintended but benign affirmation that what we sense we are missing in our spiritual lives is still missing.

And not to be found where it does not thrive and flourish, where institutional control has replace the freedom of the true spiritual encounter with the hidden splendor.

Most of us have never had an experience of the sacred within us. And no contact with teachings that can lead us to the ultimate mystery that lies within. Conventional religious traditions tend to dismiss the mystical experience, but that is really the purpose with which they ought to be engaged.

If those earthly authorities claim that mysticism is only meant for the elite few, who and what is the spiritual authority behind that claim. And who are the elite for whom the inner teachings are meant.

There is an eastern saying that when the student is ready the teacher, or perhaps the teachings, will appear. But then, how does the student, the spiritual aspirant, prepare himself or herself for the next step in their spiritual education.

There still exist spiritual traditions in which individuals with aspirations to advanced self-knowledge along spiritual lines of inquiry are trained in techniques of self-transcendence. And monitored by advanced adepts so that they do not deviate from their chosen path or mistakenly interpret inner experiences for something other than what they are.

The ego is always determined to assert its preferences, and until it can be brought under conscious control by the witness-observer within it will generally present itself as the inner filter through which we should see our lives.

To an advanced spiritual adept, living under the imaginative spell and daily control of the ego is mere childishness, with a retarding effect on our psychological and spiritual growth. We must first learn to recognize the ways in which the ego acts on our conscious decision-making processes. And then learn to overcome its influence and take charge of our own conscious evolution.

This is no easy task if we are not prepared to deny the ego access to the standard roles it assigns itself in the management of our affairs. And to which we almost automatically give over our consent.

If we are to behave as conscious beings, as is intended, then we must be conscious of every aspect of our behavior. What we leave to chance will most likely return to haunt us when we are least prepared, or busy with other items on our inner agenda. Which may very likely create another in a seemingly endless series of unintended opportunities for us to learn the value of patience.

To do less, to avoid paying conscious and serious attention to the events on our daily agenda is to live an unexamined life, and potentially blind ourselves to the opportunities for continued growth and well-being.

And if we do this, as many of us do, we do it in error. The consequence always is that errors must eventually be recognized as such and corrected until they become the path of truth.

Not to the point of obsessive-compulsive behavior, but because of the recognition that if we want to reach the summit we will have to train hard, an arduous task, and prepare ourselves for a difficult ascent.

In that sense, a spiritual path is a profoundly serious and thorough exploration and training of individual consciousness for the purpose of understanding the roots of behavior and exploring the levels and depth of the human psyche.

Surely we should now be striving for a profoundly-objective, thorough and experiential knowledge of the structure of the human psyche. And in the same thorough manner we have learned to explore and understand all relevant areas and aspects of our physical existence. We are mountain climbers as well as plateau dwellers.

How else, in what other manner could we possibly hope to evolve past our often childish preoccupations with occasionally infantile and often disastrously destructive behavior.

We must mature as a species in the same manner that so many of us have matured as individuals. With full and conscious knowledge of our behavior, and absolute responsibility for our actions.

And yet, considering the world-wide technological destruction we have visited upon our planetary home, and the terrifying possibilities that potentially await us at the hands of so many practitioners of violence for the sake of violence, assuming conscious control over our evolution is an absolutely and imperative immediate necessity. And must proceed at a far greater pace than has traditionally occurred if we are to survive human folly.

But it is a sad truth that many of us do not, have not and never will evolve past our childish obsessions, and with the added caveat that we are in danger of becoming adults with full and ultimate responsibility for our behavior. And some of us may be unprepared for that responsibility.

Damn the torpedoes, full speed ahead! has traditionally been considered a courageous act of wartime bravery, and in that context may be admirable when danger threatens. But it is not the action of a self-aware, self-responsible matured and spiritually well-developed individual when we are at peace.

The spiritual injunction to turn the other cheek may not necessarily mean any specific form of absolute and utter passivity in the face of evil either, for most of us at least. It may have more to do with the control over the ego's sensitivities and rashness than passivity in the face of danger.

It is a useful guide when we consider lesser forms of assault, when it is our ego that is under scrutiny or threatened by adverse criticism. But not necessarily our physical existence that must go undefended. Most of us would not willingly go to the cross.

This is certainly one way in which we might further our own evolution along, through the accurate perception of the events with which we come in contact. Judging most carefully when necessary, and certainly never arbitrarily or in haste.

In that way, avoiding having to suffer any unintended consequences of acting on our mistaken perceptions. And therefore avoiding the unfortunate results of having acted without accurate information, responding to an emotional or intellectual bias, or a self-imposed categorical imperative of having unnecessarily judged at all.

How many of us have done just that, and faced up to the necessity of apologizing for our mistaken or harmful actions. Or the shame and embarrassment of being unable to do so when the ego asserts its self-justifying privileges.

We could change all that by changing the reflexive nature of our spontaneous reactions to adverse situations or potentially harmful events. We could learn to moderate our behavior and modulate our thinking, which is the be-all and end-all of any spiritual tradition.

We could rejuvenate our sense of the sacred, and endorse any activity in which we are involved in accordance with the sacredness of life and the spiritual nature of all existence. It is the way forward.

FIVE

A sense of the sacred

Modern man has placed his trust in an essentially mechanistic view of the cosmos, a universe in which all things are essentially pre-determined according to natural energy flows and the inter-action of material forces.

And all miraculously emanating from a singularity which appeared suddenly, bursting forth in the violent explosion of the Big Bang and from which poured forth the enormous energies that gradually coalesced to form the universe as we know it now. All that was, all that is, and all that ever will be.

An unacknowledged miracle of creation put forth as scientific fact, reporting a first cause without an accompanying explanation. And without supporting evidence for the miraculous accumulation of enormous forces within that singularity, other than the convenience of an opinion.

From what source or sources did those energies or gases or unknown and unevaluated materials originate, those of us without blind adherence to scientific doctrine alone might respectfully wonder. And what caused them to come together in that primal singularity.

Modern man has sold out his enlightening and sublime spiritual aspirations for the distorted version and myopic vision of a cosmos without a creative impulse or creative intelligence behind the phenomena of existence. Without the on-going influence and activities of the divine effulgence.

A universe without the inter-active guiding counsel of the spiritual domain, without the reality of the divine presence. Foolishly intent, according to the unenlightened self-regard in which modern man holds himself up as his own champion, on claiming credit and intellectual responsibility of his own account for knowledge of the cosmos and all that is in it.

A philosophy which eventually gives him, if misused, as it so often has been, unlimited license to despoil the creation for his own purposes. And his own destiny along with it.

A bloodthirsty quarterization of reality in which spirit is ignored, mocked or denied, and the pale enchantments of materialistic thinking and the conventional activities of physical being capture our imagination and our will.

And in the ensuing process, controls the ebb and flow of mental activities to the exclusion of the sublime, spiritual aspects of the incredible gift of life. Inevitably leading, without the influence of the creative impulse of spirit, to an unstoppable suicide of the will through the loss of creative imagination and a self-destructive failure of nerve.

We are beginning to recognize this now, many of us, and long for the re-introduction of genuine spirituality and the truly religious experience, freed from cant and ritualization, in our contemporary ways of thinking and being. Not by turning our backs on the collective achievements of the past, but by building on it and looking forward to future possibilities.

A subtle but underground consensus is rapidly growing that spirituality is the true core of religious belief, and the mainstay of common discourse. This is one way that change is accelerating in the contemporary standards that reject conventional medieval descriptions of the spiritual realm as the essential underpinnings of existence.

Religious traditions and belief systems abound that substitute organized non-experiential formats that paradoxically reject the mystical approach to religious teachings and existence itself. And then deny their followers access to any teachings or techniques that can lead to a direct experience of the spiritual realm, and an ensuing mystical embrace of the cosmos. Paradoxes abound in the Land of Nod.

It may be too late for some of us to change the standard song we have been trained to sing, now that time and tide have forced the orchestra to stop playing due to age or indifference.

But the rest of us still have a chance to move on and ahead with our spiritual aspirations. The muse we listen to in that regard is the music of the spheres throughout eternity, and evolution is the song they sing.

To honor and respect the achievements of past cultures is admirable, a deserving testament to their efforts to live while they are still alive and die in accord with the divine. That was their way, and we should build on that and create our own.

Each age must write its own books, wrote Ralph Waldo Emerson with prophetic insight. To be eternally bound by the thinking of long-since vanished eras can only result in stagnation of the mind, a dulled and featureless imagination, and inevitably, eventually leading to the denial of our spiritual nature. Unless we excavate the truth of those teachings, and incorporate it into our own thinking.

This is absolutely necessary in an evolving civilization and a growing universe, avoiding the death of innovation and the imperial road to extinction. Rote thinking leads to a philosophical and spiritual dead-end in a cosmos vibrantly alive with endless possibilities.

Whose song should we be singing in so nearly an infinite universe. The song of past peoples and ancient civilizations, whose other achievements we have generally long since surpassed. Or the song of life, which beckons us to explore its nuances and the inherent possibilities of consciousness itself.

We know so little but assume so much in that regard. Without even knowing what consciousness is or how it and we ourselves came into being, we defer serious attention from this profound riddle of existence by relying on past teachings and Bronze Age dogmatic theologies that do nothing to satisfy the genuine and seriously-profound pursuit of self-knowledge.

This is not in our best interests, serving neither short-term nor long-term potential goals. They barely satisfy our religious habits and standard references to spirit, and thereby only vaguely remind us of the religious traditions we have inherited.

But our modern religious customs do not fulfill the potentials inherent that our spiritual and mystical traditions point towards and seek to fulfill. At best, they merely hint at the unawakened and unexplored landscape of the inner territory of the psyche.

We are a species that has come to rely virtually alone on dualistic ancient ideas and medieval beliefs as the conflicting pathways to the future. They are nothing of the kind if they are taken as literal truths rather than what they actually are, metaphorical statements whose purpose is the realization of the inner self of mankind.

This is the core of the mystical approach, true spirituality, and it is always perceived as a threat by institutional forces to their authority, governing autonomy and overt control over their adherents in all areas of their lives.

Mysticism offers something much more than that form of borderless religious caste system, ordered along the lines of a medieval liege-lord and the inhabitants of his domain rather than along enlightening lines of spiritual freedom.

Mysticism supports an individual practitioner in the pursuit of direct experience, and the inherent possibility of personal enlightenment. And this is a reality over which no institution can assert any form of control other than through forceful means of repression or the threat of socio-religious ostracism.

Powerful enough, as far as they go, but when enough individuals band together in search of enlightened teachings, the castle walls will begin to crumble, the drawbridge begin to rot, and the castle moat will eventually be drained of water.

Nothing lasts forever, not even the most determined resistance to evolutionary progress and the forward movement to a more matured and better informed understanding of the place of mankind in the cosmos.

There are those mystically-oriented teachings from the ancient world that recognized the possibilities for evolutionary advancement along lines of the transformation of consciousness, just as there are teachings that did not.

The subject is far more complex than simple dualistic philosophies are capable of discussing in a meaningful way to an uniformed or uninterested audience. And this may be why, along with the outer level of exoteric teachings, there often developed an inner core of esoteric teachings. Duality again.

It would appear probable that the history of mankind is far older, far more ancient and complex than has previously been reported. The story of ancient man has undergone some unexpected twists in recent years, including the probability that enlightenment traditions were known and practiced in many cultures in the ancient world. And very possibly in ancient cultures, of which only scattered hints remain from recent archeological discoveries.

Archeological discoveries, such as the recently uncovered monolithic ruins at Gobekli Tepe along with the enlightening interpretations of ancient Egyptian spiritual teachings on consciousness by R. A. and Isha Schwaller de Lubicz, more properly called Khemitology, suggest that some ancients had a far more sophisticated understanding of the nature of human consciousness than do many contemporary traditions.

Other than contemporary mystical teachings, esoteric religious traditions and shamanic cultures world-wide, virtually all fundamentalist-oriented religions have little or nothing to say about human consciousness. The approach is dualistic; the orientation almost always in favor of a generally uninformed myopic reverence for an historic or semi-historic founding figure.

In a sense, those approaches to spirituality are chasing up the blind alley of religious fundamentalism. But the past cannot be resuscitated and brought back to life. And to focus on dualist thinking and the emergence of retrograde fundamentalist forces is diametrically opposed to the evolutionary impulse in man. We may mourn, but the past is gone forever.

It is a choice we make, conscious or otherwise, but not necessarily a spiritual revelation. Still, we are all entitled to our own choices and how we interpret them. We may have done the best we could with what we had. Or we night have chosen a religious default position, accepted whatever was on our plate and moved on with our lives. But not ahead.

And then again, there are those of us who firmly and whole-heartedly believe in the dualistic approach to spirituality and the attending religious tradition that is embedded in their hearts. To which they are entitled, and which may offer them the best possibilities for spiritual well-being in their immediate environment.

Who is there to judge what is best for anyone of matured years, other than what is best for oneself. And even then, we are ourselves so often filled with doubt and disillusion that it may occasionally appear that for every three steps forward we may simultaneously advance two steps to the rear.

Evolution makes no clear-cut promises about anything, and extinction is a distinct possibility for any species. By now it is clearly obvious that human evolution is fraught with peril on many levels, much of it self-imposed in recent generations.

We may be our own best friend, and we may also be our worst enemy. Such is the nature of dualism when we examine the workings of the mind and intellect. To our distress, we may find ourselves vacillating between a cosmic *Yes!* and a gawping *No!*

To know the truth one must become the truth, and this is no easy matter. And definitely far more than simply following institutional and artificial rules of existence, which many traditions insist are the sole and only basis for their version of the one and only true religion among so many other competing one and only true religions.

A huge claim that supplies those making the claim with a religious authority for which they do not usually supply the hard nutshell of attending proof. Other, that is, than through pseudo-mythic historical revelations and the inconsistency of deterministic institutional thinking masquerading as enlightenment.

There is no court of last resort to which those among us who doubt can appeal for enlightened judgment. And who cannot penetrate beyond the standard barriers that prevent us from accepting convention and tradition as anything more than what they are, Johnny-come-lately pretenders to the throne.

There is no one and no governing institution to whom or to which we can present the case for the opposition concerning the recent rise of religious fundamentalism. But that may be to our loss.

This might be the spiritual cross-roads we will all eventually reach, and must then make the decision which way to turn.

Either way, we all must find our way off the inner cross that fundamentalism extolls.

If we are oriented towards the dualistic approach to existence, we will simply look for a different path or a different religion. And then continue asking the same questions in the same manner to which we previously found no answers, and which will continue to add to our mounting frustration with spiritual concerns. We are still stuck on the Ferris Wheel instead of dancing along the Yellow Brick Road on our way to the Emerald City.

Or we might choose a different approach entirely. Instead of turning around and about, choosing a similar path except this time with different names and different symbols for the same or similar ideas and concepts, we might choose to take the non-dualistic approach and turn inward.

We might decide to seek within our being for what we assumed could only be found hidden in the depths of a strange and forbidding jungle. And which, if found, we might worship from afar but never more than that.

The mounting frustrations of the spiritual search might lead us to conclude that we have been looking in the wrong place to find that which has never been lost. We are ourselves, as we are taught by the ancient Indian Upanishadic teachings, that which we seek outside ourselves. *We are that; that we are.*

The realization of which in terms of the transformation of human consciousness presents the case for enlightenment. The self-realization of our true nature, the universal consciousness which has descended into the human template.

This is non-duality, representative of most eastern and shamanic teachings, but a far cry from the standard dualistic, fundamentalist teachings on exoteric levels of Biblical religions.

The esoteric teachings within Judaism, Christianity and Islam are not well represented in their general public formats, and are often restricted by temperament, frowned on or actively reproached to the point of critical and harsh repression, or even complete disavowal.

A wave may expend itself on reaching the shore, but it is not its own independent creation, and will inevitably be followed by other waves. It is caused by the force of the wind and ocean currents acting on the body of water.

The one who seeks after enlightenment is like that wave. Not an atypical, anomalous instance of individual initiative, but one of a large and increasing body of individuals no longer content with the dualistic approach to existence.

And seeking transcendence from the dualism of the inert religious approach that does not and cannot satisfy our spiritual hunger, neither with a wafer nor a sip of wine.

Spiritual growth requires genuine sustenance for its continued evolution, and cannot be satisfied by sentimental punctuations, stereophonic slogans, high-minded edicts, celebratory proclamations or emotional attachment to striated religious ceremonies.

Those kinds of substitutions merely turn us into passive audiences for a pseudo-spiritual activity which does not inform. And which can never satisfy our hunger for the genuine experience of spiritual transformation and self-realization.

When hungry we eat, when thirsty we drink. But the spiritual malaise that hangs so headily over the air which we breathe so painfully is a form of religious pollution that has dulled our physical and psychic senses to the joy of existence.

We have become immured to the effects they have on our being through the demeaning familiarity of contempt. And the constant hypocrisy of religious bigotry. And institutional forces as well that constantly deny the innate presence of the transforming spirituality that only comes through enlightenment. And the practice of the presence of the divine.

We are being buried under the weight of our own inadvertent hypocrisy, added to by the overwhelming force of religious repression that suffocates our curiosity and the inherent evolutionary impulse within our psychic structure to expand our conscious awareness.

We deny ourselves our own evolutionary progress when we willing reside, and therefore remain stuck in the playthings of racial immaturity. We have focused entirely too much of our attention on the exploration and exploitation of our outer environment.

But in doing that we have generally neglected the exploration of the universal consciousness which orders and informs our lives. Our innate nature is as much a mystery to us as what lies in the depths of the sea or exists beyond the heavenly lights in the starry skies.

Consciousness, as we are informed by those who have looked deeply, solemnly and experientially into the matter, the enlightened masters of mankind, is everything of value and everything worth thinking about when we consider our place in the cosmos.

Consciousness is the most profound mystery in the realm of human behavior. It is what we are, and that is our one redeeming quality. We are conscious, we are self-aware, and we are thinking creatures. We are one way in which the universe births itself and comes into material being.

Without consciousness and the life force that animates the otherwise inert biological manifestation that is the physical body, as we all know, we are merely inert forms of decaying protoplasm with no redeeming qualities. And no particular reason for existence except eventually to become food for worms and add our weight to the body of the universe.

That dismal prospect may await our material bodies, but we, the consciousness within, will not follow our bodies to that same fate. We will not end at the grave. Where we go and what we do is a matter for our mystical and spiritual traditions to explore. John Donne:

The grave's a fine and private place,
but none, I think, do there embrace.

We should all be concerned with our mortal prospects as embodied beings. And some of us are, those who have become aware of the gradual disintegration of our physical bodies as we age and suffer increasing difficult setbacks.

We may become increasingly distressed by the diminishing prospects of our current physical embodiment as the body begins to deteriorate, becoming increasingly unresponsive through age or illness.

One way or another, the reality of material existence will inevitably begin to assert its increasingly demanding presence. The accompanying rules of physical engagement will make its hard and often harsh demands on our bodies, our minds and our spirit. We no longer are what once we were. And what we will become, when the body drops away, is what should and does give us pause to consider with serious intent.

If we remain detached and unconcerned because the teachings we follow have prepared us for the gradual decay and falling away of the body, we will have an easier time of it than those who have not. It may be a difficult transition in any case, but we will benefit from a spiritual orientation when our time comes and we enter the next dimension.

Those who have not prepared themselves will likely face the fading away of the light with horror and trepidation. And when they enter succeeding realms of conscious awareness as disembodied spirits, they may feel they have entered a perpetual chamber of horrors in eternity.

Whatever the case may be, whatever the truth may be, there will inevitably come a point in our personal history when we must face these issues, even if we do so unwillingly. Why not take the bit between our teeth and take charge of the inevitable outcome of physical existence.

None of us know when that final moment will come, since none of us are guaranteed length of years and an undisturbed set period of health and well-being. This is the reality that must be faced.

So we should face it, and prepare ourselves for the approach of physical death, the great transition, while we are still alive and fully functioning. While we are still capable of understanding, evaluating and accepting the fundamental spiritual truths of our existence in conscious preparation for the afterlife.

We should seek true enlightenment about our physical existence, our mental reality and the spiritual presence within us before death makes an appearance and our time nears its end. Or before the processes of physical disentanglement from the material body due to age or infirmity begin, take their final toll and muddy up the processes of life.

And then blind us to the eternal light of full consciousness when we depart the body. Which will then force us to reside at lower levels of awareness until at some future point, in some future existence perhaps, we will be able to proceed further in our evolutionary journey.

Our various attachments to material existence and the physical body will continue to hold us back and retard our progress. We are informed by spiritual sources that we will return, again and again, to physical embodiment through the process of reincarnation. With the same or other lessons to learn until finally we pass the human course.

Our spiritual learning may be all we can ever take with us when we depart the body, and may be what sustains us when we turn within in times of stress or anxiety in each lifetime for spiritual guidance, and the inherent wisdom that our intuition reveals lies within us.

What we may be accessing when spiritual guidance and intuition do help us clear our earthly path of unexpected drawbacks and unwanted obstacles is the soul wisdom and soul knowledge we have earned from previous lifetimes.

And to which we will eventually add our own hard-earned and precious learning when we too re-unite with our soul. And the earned wisdom of this lifetime is absorbed into our greater being.

We should begin to look into this now, while we are still capable of adjusting our current attitudes and psychological approach to the significant problem that spirituality creates when we become serious about the issue.

Like begets like. And when it comes to the subject of spiritual evolution, the more we can explore and incorporate the message of spiritual transformation into our thinking, the more firmly the evolutionary nature of our being will expand our experience of life. And possibly of existence itself.

Which also means an increase in our appreciation of all other forms of life with which we share this existence. And if we look deeply enough into that appreciation, we will soon enough find a substratum of universal and infinite love that is the source of the bliss of existence.

Something that awaits us all. Something we can all experience when we search deeply enough beneath our mental presence and within our psychic being.

Divorcing ourselves from the attachment of material being, detached from personal relationships in the sense of emotional yearning and compulsive grasping, we can begin the journey towards the Grail Castle that resides within our spiritual hearts.

We must find our way through an entangled, inter-woven and dense forest like a medieval knight on a vision quest to find the Holy Grail. This is the inner psychological landscape of our personal history, immersed in and expressive of typical and atypical archetypal reactions of the human psyche to the problems of physical existence.

It is that mixture of the personal with the impersonal genetic make-up of our species with which we must contend in our inward journey towards the light. The journey to the light is what spirituality is about, and nothing else.

We must learn how to separate both subjective and objective interior strains of psychological reality, along with the inner reactions to both that help us define our being. This is a difficult but necessary adjunct in our exploration of the psychological and spiritual reality with which we must contend.

We must effectively clear the inner debris field of our mental history and psychological make-up before the clear light of a new day can make itself known and felt. But which otherwise we see only dimly, as though through a looking glass with murky lenses.

Before we can move on in our understanding of our human self, and explore the enhanced possibilities that spiritual vision enables for a clearer and more accurate understanding of the reality in which we exist.

Clear enough so that we can see and experience existence for ourselves, through the unfiltered vision of spiritual enlightenment. Without the disabling mental pressure of emotional and psychological prejudice coloring and distorting our various experiences of material reality and physical being.

We may prefer to endorse the emotional residue of past experiences and the habits of a lifetime, but that leads only to stagnation and the futility of transcendent despair.

Which is also to suggest that our understanding of the universe will continue to be myopic, alienating, distorted and adding only to our innate frustration with life. And detract from our experience of self-knowledge and self-worth.

Why should this be so when in virtually all other fields of knowledge we have made such enormously sophisticated technological strides. One reason may be that emotions are all too often overly-involved in matters of critical judgment.

When it comes to self-knowledge and the spiritual condition of humanity, many of us may simply resort to sentimentally-emotional attitudes. These erratic and often impulsive attitudes endorse a pre-mature closure of reality when critical attitudes set in intellectual cement may often affirm to our emotional sorrow.

Those old-time traditional religious conventions and attitudes with which we are all so overly familiar, with all the affiliate song and dance of seasonal merchandising and popular cultural myth-making, add nothing to our ongoing investigation of the universe.

Other than the pretext of calming our existential anxieties, which adds only another burdensome layer of pretense to our increasingly heavy-handed cultural make-up. Under which we spiritually suffocate, and which we must eventually shed before we will see the enlightening momentum of a new day.

We have contented ourselves with only an on-going rationale but no spiritual investigation or experience for our continued religious habits. Or the purposes according to and for which we observe them. This is merely stagnation, and is a misuse and misinterpretation of the reason for faith.

Faith should be used as a motivation to explore our spiritual goals and realize them within our own being. But not blandly accept whatever pseudo-spiritual fare is set before us, which we are advised and often admonished to uncritically and wholeheartedly accept as the consummation of our religious duties. Hogwash.

This is not the religious experience, it is propaganda masquerading as evidence. And would be unacceptable in any scientific undertaking, in the halls of academia, in the administrative services of governing authorities and in the general attitudes of common-sense wisdom many of us are familiar with in our daily lives.

This is not the way to lead a self-responsible, self-governing and enlightened life. It is spiritual slavery, not to a God of love and mercy, but merely to dogma and theology, the wishes and desires of governing institutional authorities, and institutional control intent on preserving its privileges and self-ordained responsibilities as would-be, self-empowered gnostic intermediaries between God and man.

We need no such institutional authorities to control our spiritual existence when we are all capable of making that direct connection for ourselves.

If we are willing to work for it. We work for everything else, but the difference is we accept that for all other things we must work to achieve our ends. Tithing an occasional tidbit to a church changes nothing of significance

We are taught that spiritual knowledge is a gift that comes to us free of charge, but only if we sign up for the course. And only if we are faithful to the institution that regulates the agenda, assigns the teachers and decides who among us has passed the exams and who have not. And what exactly would a passing grade be based on, proficiency in dogma and theology?

Along with membership dues, which appear to be never-ending and come in a variety of forms in order to sustain the over-all effort. This can be an expensive process, and some of us may one day discover that they have paid in far more than they got back.

We learn as we go along, which is certainly true as a useful generalization about human existence. But how else could it be, since when we were born none of us was given a book of instructions on how to live a decent and spiritually-enlivening human lifetime.

That learning appears to be among the primary processes and purposes of existence. The spirituality of learning that represents the thrill of variety, the decision-making activities that symbolize free will, and the mysteries of where we have come from, where we are heading, and whatever intermediary steps we may find ourselves taking along the way. The currency of life.

We are here to learn, to inform ourselves of the nature of existence on the plane of duality. To grow and mature past that stage of our existence in order to disengage ourselves from our obsessive and compulsive attachment to the material expression of being.

It is *that* obsession which pulls us back, lifetime after lifetime, to express ourselves in terms of material reality. Physical reality is thrilling in its own way, but it is the addiction to physical existence that compels us to regard it as the one and only reality to which we can adhere.

Most of us cannot conceive of or identify with the experience of disembodied existence as beings of light and energy. Our human imaginations are unequal to the task of envisioning a state of being that exists beyond our human form and capabilities.

Since we have no conscious experience of that it is understandable that we are unable to think in those terms, but there are those who can and do. We speak their names with reverence, but dimly and from a distance.

We may admire the attainment of enlightened beings to higher states of consciousness, but many of us dare not seek their company. We imagine, or are taught, that their existence speaks to a divine order of being, an act of grace or some supernatural visitation, rather than the achievement of the ultimate aim of human existence.

Some of us are taught that, born in sin and conceived in guilt, we are doomed by our innately fallen nature to a lesser state of existence. Hogwash again, and nothing less.

We are denied the rightful, willful and purposeful ascent of our own consciousness by individuals, institutions and teachings that seem absolutely intent on preserving and protecting their historic territory, rather than seeking out new ways of exploring that territory and passing that learning along. Or receiving it anew.

Or uncovering new territories to explore. The conventional and traditional spiritual imagination has reached the dead-end of its inherent stagnation, intent on preserving the past rather than anticipating the future.

With nowhere to go in that regard except through the failed time machines of religious rites and rituals, trying to recreate what never was, and re-invigorate that which has long since passed on into the dead weight of history.

Spirituality is the living experience of conscious existence, but religion, in its fundamentalist aspect, tends to ignore the exploration, understanding and expansion of consciousness to concentrate its efforts on worshipping its only imagined versions of past events.

In this way religion betrays the fundamental reason for its existence. One way of regarding the meaning of the word religion is to consider the mystical inspiration of its root form in Latin, religio. A spiritually-inspired definition suggests the concept of "linking back," rejoining the subjective, individual phenomenal consciousness to the universal consciousness, that which we traditionally call God.

This is the mystic approach, the meaning and purpose of enlightenment, and it should be what religion ought to be concerned with rendering. But does not because it cannot. Those who formally represent religious institutions cannot teach what they do not know themselves.

And in that ignorance lies their undoing. Religions that do not seek to ascend to the highest levels of human attainment are ultimately doomed to fail, cut off at the knees for their failure to achieve their purpose.

Which, again, is to reunite individual consciousness with the greater consciousness of which we are all an individual manifestation. What mystics have achieved, those upon whose life and teachings those religions were built and now maintain, is the real teaching, the only religious teaching that truly advances our evolutionary journey.

Mysticism is a difficult teaching, of course it is. It is transforming and inviolate under the terms of its own existence. There are no shortcuts to enlightenment. What is involved is the total transformation of human consciousness, and from that there is no retreat, no ephemeral rites or rituals, no holding back from direct and total participation.

It will proceed at its own pace, although great effort is called for and the rewards may not always be immediately apparent. Faith is crucial, but one must work hard for the attainment.

What sets the intense and isolating effort of transforming one's own consciousness apart from all other human endeavors is that it cannot be done for the sake of ego enhancement. Or to set the individual apart from, and higher than his contemporaries.

Money, fame, success or acclaim play no role in the difficult and vital work of exploring and mastering the inner processes of the mind. Along with the extraordinary difficulty of taming the ego in order to allow the greater light of divine consciousness to illuminate our inner being.

In this regard, one might consider that the whole of our inner existence is merely a loosely-knit fabrication, a construction in consciousness that we ourselves have developed and maintained over the course of our lives. The illusion for which we are prepared to go to war each time we imagine it is threatened or under scrutiny.

A finite version of our infinite self. Not something essentially intrinsic to our being, but an artificial self with which we identify. Constantly changing according to changing circumstances. Always unhappily on the alert for any sign of tell-tale change that threatens the inherently unstable structure of our already frail ego. And the persona, the false self with which we identify.

A totally made-up creation, constantly justifying its existence with death-defying rattles each time it veers off course, and we are caught up in a train wreck that real or imagined, temporarily or otherwise, threatens to derail our life.

We tend to live according to those transitory details, phantom-like in their origins and often vanishing quickly in the blink of an eye. But we also tend to ignore the witness-observer aspect of our consciousness, whose existence functions according to the rules and conditions of a different order of reality.

A part of our being is always aware of the spiritual realm and often, one way or another, in direct or indirect contact. But the bulk of our awareness is focused on the here and now business of our lives.

A greater balance is needed if we are ever to move past the only-assumed limitations we have accepted as a fundamental condition of our spiritual existence. It is not. It is only a habit we have developed over time, a tradition of human existence which we have accepted as the truthful rendition of our mortal existence.

This is nothing more than an existential Hail Mary pass we have hurled off into the universe hoping for a favorable response. It is ignorance being passed off as reality, and we should not let our ignorance take office and rule the inner landscape of our being.

Wisdom cannot flourish when we are ruled by ignorance. We ought finally to recognize how essentially ignorant most of us are when it comes to our spiritual identity. And along with that, the possibilities for transforming our state of consciousness to more enhanced and evolved states of being.

Some of us may be thinking more along the lines of what we might have to lose rather than what we have to gain. But that is just ignorance shaping a traditional fear of change, and cannot bear scrutiny once we have educated ourselves about the processes of spiritual growth and maturation.

The only thing we have to lose is the fear of loss, but what we will have lost will only be the imaginary fears that all too often we have allowed to define our existence. We have been spooked by things that occasionally go bump in the night.

Which is another reason for the time-honored spiritual injunction to awaken from the illusions we have created ourselves. We live under the gray and cloudy shadowy skies that only dimly-illuminate our existence.

Awaken, dear ones, the ancient eastern teachings acclaim. And those who hear the call become restless when they cannot fall back to sleep. Those who do not hear and do not see fall back quickly and easily into the waking dream of illusion.

When one has truly heard the call of spirit one cannot return to a life that was, and an existence consciously known to be devoid of soul. There is no substitute for truth. There is nothing that can turn us away from spiritual wisdom when we have had the direct experience that such a possibility exists.

And it does. It is our birthright and our heritage. It belongs to us and we to it. We ought to make use of this precious human lifetime to acquaint ourselves intimately and consciously with the spiritual truth of our existence.

There is always a choice, but in truth, once we awaken from the dream of material existence and physical reality there is no choice. We are not victims of chance or the fickleness of fate, we are the universe dreaming itself into being.

We are that, the immortal nature of our being and not the nightmare we imagine is our mortal existence. Death is a transition from one state of being to another, not the ultimate ending we fear. We should deal with these primal fears rather than yield to the terrifying scenarios many of us imagine will one day, sooner or later, be heading our way.

We always have a choice. We can live in alienation and isolation when we live under the shadow of fear. Or we can illuminate our being when we find the true sun of our existence, the enlightenment of spiritual illumination within our being. We should choose wisely and with courage. We are the only visible authority to whom we should report.

Six

We should choose wisely

We should choose wisely or suffer the consequences of whatever default position it is that reflects the arbitrariness of the cloud of unknowing that floats over us on an otherwise cloudless day.

And casts its shadow over our lives when we yield personal control over to whatever unnamed or unnamable forces dictate the politics of our lives. Which is the consequence of not choosing well or wisely.

We are taught that we must take whatever we are given, accept whatever we are told, and go wherever the prevailing winds blow. Belief is no longer a choice but a matter of eminent domain.

Instead of ruling our private kingdoms according to our own skills and devices, kings of our own castles and rulers of our own domains, we have become vassal serfs instead in a landscape which is no longer familiar and a land which is no longer our own.

Pawns we are becoming in a system that favors the rich and powerful exclusively, ruled by governing authorities whose loyalties have long-since been bought and paid for. And a population now afflicted with widespread and pervasive spiritual malaise.

We are becoming a stricken and torn-apart society in which the seven deadly sins have found safe harbor under the guise of sham populist rhetoric. No culture can long survive a determined attack on its moral underpinnings, and a deteriorating general sense of what is acceptable and what is not. Morality becomes a matter of political expediency.

When we are no longer able to tell the difference between truth and political talking points, we accept the professional lies of professional spin doctors. An abominable phrase and an even more abominable profession.

Their job is to convince us that when it is dark out it does not necessarily mean the sun isn't shining in some other location. Just not on us, which means it isn't dark everywhere. The non-answer is being passed off as a generalized truth. Everything is relative now, especially including truth.

Not exactly a direct lie, but certainly a deflection of attention from the truth of a particular situation. In this case, the particular truth is that the sun isn't shining because it is evening. And similarly, when we do not choose wisely our attention is always, one way or another, being deflected from the truth.

After enough time has passed living, or simply existing, in the shadows of darkening clouds of ignorance and despair, we may no longer be able to tell day from night, light from dark, sunshine from shadow.

We may be in danger of becoming a population of sheep with only occasionally scattered Internet references to the dangers that confront us as a free people, living amid the plight of a democracy when power and greed take the helm of the ship of state.

When we stop attending to the ship properly it will eventually begin to leak, then more leaking seams will inevitably make an appearance. Water will eventually fill the hold, the ship will flood, capsize and sink.

The same thing happens to civilizations when they begin to rot from within. They sink under the weight of their own misdeeds, their own hypocrisies, and their own lawless class of white collar criminals freed by money and power from an overly-active moral conscience.

With laws, and lawmakers, whose silence can be purchased. Which effectively means no laws and no conscience left to guide the ruling powers. And consequently, morality is given an indefinite and unpaid leave of absence.

White collar criminals come prepared with accountants and lawyers, pockets filled with politicians and gold. When they rise to the top, a society or culture can become top-heavy with greed and corruption on every level.

And which then topples over with a shock heard round the world, including the delicate sensitivities of those individuals too attentive to their own needs to see the overall danger that threatens the continued health and well-being of themselves, their families and their comrades without arms.

Corruption always tends to suffocate the powerless majority who bear the economic brunt of the disastrous consequences when a society begins to go wrong and veers off track. A society that carries the weight of economic and military power heavily, without moderation, without humility and without justice for all cannot long survive the attacks of internal and external enemies who have had enough, and seek revenge.

And especially so when the ruling elite are without the redeeming qualities of compassion for those who are suffering, sympathy for the disabled, empathy for the unfortunate, and the obligations of the fortunate few for their less well-off brothers and sisters, their fellow beings and comrades in arms.

This is when a culture is in denial of its spiritual hopes and aspirations, willfully ignorant of the immeasurable reality of the creative intelligence that dominates the inner landscape of our individual and collective being.

This is when the movement towards spiritual presence begins to suffer from the mockery of the spiritless, the corruptions of institutional power, and the distempered, repressive and reactionary visitations of religious authoritarians set against those who seek their own experience of the divine.

Not for nothing are spiritual movements driven underground, taking shelter from persecution when repressive, reactionary forces begin their inquisitions anew. The toll can be enormous when repression becomes the new order of a new day.

And any inquisition, far from being a merely historic footnote to a more intolerant time, is almost always in the hearts and minds of those who seek to impose their own distorted visions of reality on the world around them. By any means available to them, whatever the cost to others may be.

We should choose wisely, and we should make our choices dictated by accurate and informed information. But not according to the talking points of talking heads on network news, cable programming or other locations that offer up only pre-digested pablum.

Or according to Internet mediocrities whose light-weight, distorted and wildly speculative neo-sociopathic ramblings justify and explain nothing, inconsequential at best, dangerous if taken seriously or acted on, and absolutely not subject to serious consideration.

We should use our free will in a matured and educated manner, which should not be news to any of us. And clearly not in the manner of any ill-informed lout with access to the Internet whose innate and general frustration with life dictates the majority of his, or her, opinions.

Free will is not quite as free as we might think once we consider the enormous repercussions and consequences of decisions made in haste or for all the wrong reasons. People have a right to their own opinions, but if we are listening we should be careful that our own sense of discrimination has not temporarily taken a leave of absence from factual history or moral considerations.

There is a price we might have to pay for an ill-considered choice, just as there are rewards we might reap from matured and thoughtful decisions. At the very least, our conscience will be at peace, our morality uplifted, and our sense of what is right will be justified by the rightful decisions we have made and the thoughtful actions we have taken.

These ideas do not exist in a vacuum, or in a universe of their own making. They are inherent in the lives we all lead in a free society. They are in the fabric of the cultural identity of educated, informed and thoughtful individuals.

They are in the air we breathe, the clothes we wear, the foods we eat and the reasons we eat them. Those ideals inform our thoughts, enlighten our attitudes, and guide our actions.

Everything we are is ultimately the result of the choices we have made. And if we are to accept responsibility for them and lead our lives in our own way, we should first rid ourselves of any fraudulent notions that everything is for the best in this best of all possible worlds.

Just as we should rid ourselves of any fraudulent arguments to the contrary. Why fraudulent? Because if we have not judged life according to our own experiences, where relevant, and if we have adopted a belief system merely because it is convenient or socially acceptable, we are living inauthentic lives based on the ease of social acceptability. But nevertheless spiritually negligent. We should make up our minds based on absolute truth, and absolutely nothing else.

We are not living our own lives if we simply go along to get along. We are living lives dictated to us by others, and this denies us rightful access to our own religious birthright and spiritual heritage.

If we are inauthentic to ourselves we cannot be true to the ideals and concepts that sustain our spiritual efforts when we turn inward, and search deeply within for the divine light of conscious illumination.

We must clear the debris field of memory, longing and desire, sorrow and regret, reflections and obsessions that characterize our struggle to survive before we can move deeply into our most truly profound inner nature and being.

There are ways of doing that, just as there still exist traditions and practices that focus on the inner life of man. Genuine spiritual traditions do everything possible to reframe the debate between mind and spirit, ego and conscious choice.

The teachings of enlightened presence are intent on escaping from the binding accoutrements of obsessive attachment to material possessions and the addictive nature and physicality of existence.

Especially including the various attachments we have to physical pleasure, along with the nearly endless demands of ego-oriented forms of domination over the all and everything of existence.

All of which cast their own darkling shadows over the individual and collective will, clouding the transformational effort and making us all susceptible to the inner eye of doubt and disbelief.

What do we really know about the spiritual reality in which some us believe part-time, others doubt or deny full-time, and which still others, a silent majority perhaps, who have not yet made up their minds or done anything to dispel their illusions or confusions.

What in this or any other world are we waiting for? Is not the subject of the nature and origin of human consciousness and the divine authorship of this creation not thought worthy enough for genuine and extended consideration.

How long does it actually take before it finally begins to sink in that we no longer know what we are talking about when we talk about God. Or the mystery of His supposed relations.

We cannot take courage from our convictions if we have none. No convictions, that is. And if we have no courage in this matter we also cannot speak with certainty about this, that, or any other thing.

Or any pretended sense of closure, that the matter is settled, over and done with because of the advance of technology and the triumph of science over religion. The consequence being that the God metaphor has finally been laid to rest. It has not, and the creative spirit that orders the universe is not simply a metaphor of no substantial value.

Perhaps an ancient or medieval concept of the divine may have bitten the dust in the Halls of Eternity, but the divine intelligence that informs the universe is alive and well, as is the creation.

And living in the most unexpected of places, without the benevolent guidance of professional skeptics and rational de-bunkers. They were not there at the creation, as the Book of Job reminds us. If they had, we might never have had it, not even as much as a sausage.

If the material reductionists had had their way, had they been there, creation might never have taken place without corroborating evidence to justify the effort and expense. And a workable economic theory to anticipate the financial costs and benefits.

Nonsensical though this may be, yet how far removed from these off-road considerations are the uninformed and immature attacks against a reliable spiritual perspective from which to guide our existence.

The rise of premature conclusions about reality decrees the death of the inquiring mind, and the premature closure of reality. All too often the first consideration inevitably is forced to be the profit motive.

Who will pay for the research and how will they financially benefit from the support of any effort that potentially may add some as yet unknown factor to human knowledge.

This is the unfortunate nature of our economic system, by which we live or die, rather than the advance of pure knowledge for its own sake in our ongoing exploration of ourselves and the universe.

Most of us do not generally consider our spiritual lives with the same earnest and daily seriousness as we lead our lives of financial striving and similar endeavors. Economics directly has to do with maintaining the health and well-being of our physical bodies, and is highest on our list of earthly priorities.

Spirituality is seen as a leisure-time activity with no discernible benefits. But spirituality has to do with the state of our soul, and that is usually not something that concerns us on a daily basis. It should of course, but the truth is far different.

Not that we are necessarily hypocritical or untrue to our religious beliefs, only that we may not place the same emphasis on our spiritual salvation as the greater regard we may have for the size of our bank accounts and the contents of our financial portfolios.

There is a certain safety in those things, in the acquisition of wealth and property, and that is certainly a necessary aspect of the human experience. But it is not the whole of the adventure.

Our investments and ownership of material possessions does not encapsulate the whole of the human experience, neither the reason nor the rewards of a human lifetime of striving and endeavor.

We have not evolved so far for the purpose of increasing our self-interests simply through the accumulation of wealth and property. The serious reward of a human lifetime comes when we have advanced our consciousness beyond the limitations of the ego-mind.

The mind and ego are necessary tools for survival, but the survival of the body is usually what is at stake for most of us, not the evolution of our soul. This is crucial to our understanding of existence and human behavior.

We automatically function according to the unwritten natural laws of survival, often without conscious control other than whatever is dictated by our experience of mundane reality.

This is clearly necessary for survival in a world of harsh extremes. But as our evolution proceeds we become more and more aware that it is not we who are in charge of the universe, but something greater within us that dictates the necessity terms of our surrender to the imprisoned splendor.

Our efforts to improve the physical nature of our existence are not matched by our efforts to explore the spiritual nature of life. And of the two, which one will we be thinking about in our last moments of conscious existence in this lifetime.

Who among us will be wishing he had spent more time in the office when he is breathing his last, or thinking about stock yields and financial investments. When the finality of death makes its presence known and deeply felt, we will all be thinking about what happens next. Or if there is anything we could have done to prepare ourselves for the final moment.

And if there is something yet to come, will we be looking forward to the adventure with courage and enthusiasm, or unhappily looking back in regret. We may put off seriously thinking about this because it is too far ahead in the far-off and distant future, we hope. Or too gloomy for the current state of our mental awareness and eager anticipation of future prospects.

Looking back at the past or thinking about the future, but both are only imaginary states of being. We can live in neither, but neither can we live in the present moment if our best efforts are spent in recalling the past and imagining the future.

We cannot imagine what death or a possible after-life state might be But instead of ignoring the mortality of existence which in this sense threatens us all, ought we not look into the matter with the same devotion that we attend to our shopping lists?

If we are not satisfied with conventional religious responses, whatever they may be, that strongly suggests we might also have to shoulder the burden ourselves and begin our spiritual education on our own.

Many of us have been completely indoctrinated into the medieval idea that the only way to salvation is through a religious institution with some particular supernatural affiliation. Any other choice would be a grievous error and the royal road to Hell.

Similar perhaps to a stock market trader enthusiastically trying to sell a particular stock to a reluctant customer, then when he makes the sale adding a disclaimer in very small print indeed that they make a market in those securities. Buyer beware.

The hellish part comes when the stock drops 50 points over a two month period, but the stock trader and his associates have long since divested themselves of their holdings, after they secured the market that they themselves created for that stock. And then taken the profits home to their banks.

A legal transfer of wealth, but the customer complaining at the bar of justice has only his own avarice and greed to blame for blinding him to reality. *There's a sucker born every minute,* an observation on American gullibility often attributed to P. T. Barnum, to which Mark Twain added, *and two to trick him.* So what else is new?

And then the process of legal tomfoolery, otherwise known as business as usual, begins all over again, and again, and yet again. But all the while the gullible among us keep placing bet after bet on the table, never knowing that the roulette wheel has been rigged and not in our favor.

I respect faith, said the legendary wit Wilson Mizner, *but doubt is what gets you an education.* And we should all be educated when it comes to matters of faith, particularly when the answers we get from religious authorities do not comfortably align with the questions we ask.

We should either ask serious questions in a louder voice, or start listening to those who do. Many, many questions, as the situation allows. We will usually be offered only enough of an answer, or non-answer as the case may be, to satisfy only those without a follow-up question in mind. Or if they do, lack the courage to ask it.

If that is the kind of tenuous spiritual education we are used to receiving, failure will very likely go to our heads. Our minds and then hearts will suffer from a surplus of unasked questions, or agonize over trite and clichéd answers. This adds nothing to an informing and inspiring knowledge of our spiritual nature. Stagnation masquerading as a press conference.

There will be no effective rationale to invoke for comfort and security when we are plagued by dark dreams that haunt us during a restless night. And there will be no escaping the lamentable fact that we did not increase our knowledge, understanding and experience of the spiritual realm because of a failure of nerve and lack of initiative.

Courage may be in short supply when we set ourselves on a haphazard educational course that may on occasion or semi-permanent basis veer off from traditional forms of religious persuasion.

But how else can we ever learn anything other than by questioning authority. And we will most likely come into direct conflict with formal religious authorities and informal enthusiasts. And what of it?

If we do not ask inconvenient questions of conventional authorities, and then question the answers we are given when they are questionable responses, we condemn ourselves to living in the mental haze of perpetual doubt and spiritual disarray. To re-frame what Hamlet says in a different context, 'tis a consummation devoutly *not* to be wished.

We would be living an unexamined existence, and consequently an inauthentic life. True faith and genuine spiritual experience will never ignite from the featureless, faithless and insubstantial sleep of illusion. No bread will ever bake from that dough.

We will have to shakes to pieces the dream state which has hypnotized our imaginative and interpretive faculties, and dulled us into critical dysfunction and spiritual impotence. And then we will have to find a way to awaken from the spiritless slumber which has taken control of both the individual and collective will towards the light.

In this sense, we must do violence towards whatever forms apathy and sloth assume that inhibit our spiritual drive, and retard the evolutionary thrust towards an enlightened understanding of our true nature.

This is an extraordinary undertaking for a spiritual aspirant in the beginning stages of a spiritual search, without direct guidance and nothing much more than an inherent sense that we have lost something of fundamental importance in this modern age of dispirited existence.

But it is perhaps little more than a spiritual fantasy for others, those who are content to remain safely within the spiritual limitations of mundane existence. Conventionally religious they may be, but they are well within the comfort zone of the relatively inert state of traditional belief.

It would be a grave error for anyone to insist that the center of gravity of conventional believers, or conventional non-believers, should be forcibly uprooted. Substituting a different belief system in which they do not believe, and which could not inspire them to further efforts within their current state of awareness will produce nothing of value. The gates of heaven cannot be stormed, and forced conversions are spiritually dead and a violation of free will.

We all evolve and grow in our own time and our own way, and that is because of the free will most of us enjoy. Consequently a genuine turn towards spirituality cannot be forced and most likely will only be delayed for another season.

And especially not for the rational supremacist, whose beliefs could not easily be uprooted from his stubborn faith in the imminent availability, power and rational exegesis of the material domain.

Acquiescence to a higher power, a divine reality, would throw over the rational supremacist, whose reliance solely on reason and logic to explain his being is a fundamental limitation in his understanding and exploration of reality.

The concept of divine inspiration, or any concordance with the divine, is antagonistic to the logical positivist's belief in reason and logic alone to explain the all and everything of material existence. The part which pretends to be the whole can never explain the whole, and is all too often reluctant to admit its failure due to mistaken allegiance in a lost cause.

There is no divine principle of existence or spiritual accord in the metaphysical vocabulary of the material reductionist. There is, in fact, no metaphysical awareness at all in the conscious vocabulary of any rational skeptic or logical exegist.

Nor in the awareness of professional cynics, who, along with the multitude of pay-for-play amateur de-bunkers, make their various ways along contemporary venues of the lecture circuit. And in spite of what they claim about the lack of evidence for religious or spiritual belief, there is no evidence for their positions according to their own terms of agreement.

Where is the proof for what they claim, that there is no guiding spirit in the cosmos, aside from shallow attacks on religious texts from a literalist and semi-informed point of view. And these are texts which they usually neither understand nor experience in terms of the metaphoric and spiritual message they reveal.

By analogy, great literature teaches us that while stories may be fictional, the reality behind them, the psychological, sociological, and yes, even the spiritual message is as real as the ground we walk on or the air we breathe.

Literature, as Nathaniel Hawthorne suggested, is a realm in which the real and the imaginary may meet. But that does not suggest that the imaginary does not represent a reality of its own.

Or that the effect it produces in us is neither substantial nor of lasting value. When we are hungry we eat, but there is a kind of hunger that cannot be satisfied by the things of this world.

The literalist can never understand the value of teaching through any method other than logical analysis. But logic alone does not usually make the heart beat faster, cannot be counted on to inspire the imagination, and does not always leave us with a sense of the sublime majesty of the cosmos.

And yet the rational supremacist clings to his skepticism and disbelief with the unearned confidence of a gambler holding a broken flush in his hand, about to see his winnings swept away by the fellow sitting across from him with a quietly discernible sense of confidence. But nevertheless bluffing with a pair of deuces.

Whichever hand wins, nothing of substantial value will be gained except the pot, which will go back on the table with the next hand, the next deal, the next turn of the wheel or the next roll of the dice. Gambling is a game of loss and losers, but in the game of life bluffing never wins the pot.

Any foolish inconsistency that gambles with life's promises as a philosophy of existence will inevitably lead to nothing of lasting value, encouraging instead the increasingly motiveless momentums of dullness and inertia, frustration and despair.

No civilization can thrive when this occurs on a widespread enough scale, as may now be well under way. History is littered with decaying ruins, replete with the shattered remnants of earnest cultures that rose quickly, and decaying civilizations that fell of their own dead weight.

For one reason or another, they could not survive their history. Will we? Which one is the anomaly, we or the factual evidence of human history? We are guaranteed nothing in this life, not another day, not another hour, not another breath. Each day, each hour, each moment could be our last.

We should honor this by remembering it, and living according to the teachings that evaluate the finite nature of material existence. Not living in fear of the unknown and what next may come our way when we eventually breathe our last, but according to a more enthusiastic and heart-felt response to the glory of the cosmos.

The possibilities our spiritual traditions have revealed await us in our present life and future incarnations, and ought to give us confidence in the true nature of the universe and our own consciousness. Death is not a permanent end, it is a transition from one state of being to another.

Who would want to continue living in a human body that has been severely corrupted by time and debilitating illness. When the infirmities of advanced age and disempowering illness have left us only a pale shadow of what once we were and can no longer be again, it is clearly time to move on.

We outgrow everything that once we clung to as we grew and matured, and that includes the body as well. Those who doubt and deny incarnation, and maintain that our existence is a one-time only affair are entitled to their convictions, but have no actual proof for their beliefs.

That is not scientific thinking, as some may claim. It is only personal opinion masquerading as a reasonable, logical and informed description of reality. Informed by what, we might inquire, since there is no proof for what is, after all, only a guess, and not even an educated one at that.

It is a materialistic orientation, prematurely prejudiced about life and existence, and against a belief in either an afterlife or the spiritual realm. Life is judged by its effects in their dream scenario, not as the result and continuing expression of a first cause, which is always denied.

Except in the case of the Big Bang theory, in which the first cause it only vaguely suggests is an expression of physical energies already magically existent. Which satisfies no logical method of inquiry without the inclusion of a free miracle inherent in the theory. Creation came about because of the forces already present in creation?

Honestly! This is judgment by those who are not equipped with enough information to judge, at the very least according to their own methods of experimental and verifiable evidence. *Show me the money!*

We are a species, as has all other species they maintain, that is the happy recipient of a fortunate chance meeting of molecules and the resulting enabling of conscious experience. *Prove it.*

In one sense, some of us may think of ourselves as a species that has created itself. This may satisfy a mind whose existence is all that is needed to explain its presence on earth, and needs no outside cause to authorize its independence or modify its egotism.

But such a false philosophical statement of being can only give rise to and empower an inherent sense of egotism no matter how it is disguised. And inevitably lead to the mindless pursuit of whatever pleasures and impulses the self-oriented mind may haphazardly experience within its interior landscape.

This is the trap that material man sets for himself when he enters the arena of self-analytical philosophical inquiry. He judges only by what he can see or experience, and thus no higher calling will be experienced or acted on.

Materialistic philosophy cannot lead to a fruitful encounter between the physical realm and the spiritual domain, since the existence of materialistic philosophy denies the existence of any other dimension of being. And will not recognize the trap it has set for itself.

Logical positivism and its allies, associates and adherents have simply defined God and the spiritual realm out of existence, since according to their definitions of reality neither can exist. The problem is, both do. Calling the tail of a cow a leg does not make it a leg. It is still a tail.

And claiming that the divine intelligence of the cosmos does not exist because it is without material form and cannot be seen is a whale of a tale. The divine may not be seen according to sensory phenomena, but that does not mean it cannot be experienced.

Because it can, it always has been and always will be available to those with eyes to see and ears to hear. Not the chosen few, according to some imaginary list of the spiritual elite, but the few who choose.

One should not look for God in the things of this world, in material forms that is, or in architectural and artistic monuments. They are only representations of the divine presence, meant to keep us alive and aware of the creative spirit. A source of imagination and enthusiasm, but not *the* source.

What we want to experience lies within, occasioned perhaps by some exterior event, but captured within the spiritual heart and experienced by the observing immortal witness-consciousness that is our true nature and to which we report in our meditations and prayer vigils.

Spiritual man, not physical man, is the means of constantly achieving the celestial vision or experience. One is taught according to one's ability to learn, and what we experience of the spiritual nature of our existence is dependent on our willingness to open to the divine within us. Like attracts like as surely in the spiritual domain as it does in the physical realm.

We are what we are, and if we listen carefully to the ancient eastern traditions they teach us that *we are that*, we *are the mystery we seek to know*. We are one collective voice among many in the universe. The universe evolving into the human form of sentient existence. The universe giving birth to itself. *We are that. We are the mystery we seek to know.*

Nothing less than that enlightened understanding and experience of our reason for being here, and the conditions of our spiritual nature, will ever satisfy the rational mind's questioning of existence. Nothing less than the direct and informing experience of the bliss of self-aware existence, along with the recognizable joy of the divine presence will ever calm a restless mind in pursuit of closure.

A closure that will never come about because of the mistaken, confusing and inconsistent adherence to reason and logic alone. Inadequately assumed to be the only reliable means of piercing through the illusions that mask humanity's true identity. The royal road to enlightenment is simply a question of identity.

The experience of enlightenment will take us past any stop-gap philosophy that attempts to plug up miscellaneous metaphysical holes by denying the holes even or ever existed. Defining them out of existence through the power of flawed reason and pseudo-logic does not mean they no longer exist, only that according to a prejudiced definition of reality they no longer can exist.

But they nevertheless remain, and generation after generation comes and goes, all asking the same fundamental questions about existence. And the questions about our own identity in the vast immensity of space.

Some ask those questions quietly of themselves in the privacy of their own minds for fear of censure. Others out loud, in a public arena. The questions of identity still continue to plague our metaphysical inquiries and confuse our minds in spite of our best efforts to wipe the slate clean and start all over again with less on our plate to deal with.

But this is an impossible task. We cannot deny the impulse to question reality, and the pseudo-religious shell-game some of us have bought into that denies us any rightful inquiry into the nature of existence.

If we buy into the conventional religious market-place of institutional thinking and institutional control, we are merely lambs being led to the metaphysical slaughter. And what is being destroyed is the will to the light whose incipient existence lies unawakened within many of us.

As long as we accept substitutions for the truly religious experience, and deny ourselves a deep, inner connection to source, we will always live in the chattel-fields that litter our existence, marked by spiritual ignorance and managed by institutional control.

This is not freedom. It does not offer us a safe religious haven from fear, or a secure sinecure from doubt and disbelief. It offers us little more than sentimental attachments to ancient religious traditions over which scholars and researchers have picked the bones clean.

We could easily become better informed now, more aware and more accepting of genuine historical researches freed from religious distortion and institutional exaggeration. Which also concurrently suggests that we will have to adapt the surface levels of our thinking to process new information and discoveries that help unclog the accumulated debris our mental habits continually leave in their wake.

We must therefore free ourselves from the intellectual and emotional sterility of cant, hypocrisy and sanctimonious babble that has infiltrated our cultural thinking. We may generally take them for useful information, but they are often nothing much more than mental clutter that clogs up the thinking process.

The mental habits of religious assumptions into which we have been indoctrinated for generations represent what we have only assumed is spiritual truth. But which, in truth, are only mythically-inspired patterns of nostalgic thought that have established habitual long-term residence in the religious atmosphere in which we live.

And consequently within our conscious awareness, and to such an extent that many of us are unable to consider any possibilities that do not fall under the spectre of the shadowy-presence they cast over our cultural identity. When we question our identity with these considerations in mind we may find ourselves sitting before a brick wall without a cementing mixture to re-inforce the coherency of the structure.

We might also discover, on the close examination that meditation on a theme brings into our awareness, the realization that each brick is only another assumption about life we have mistakenly assumed is an unshakeable truth. But it, and they, are not. They are only a diverse mixture of assumptions we have loosely bound together in the futile hope that somehow, in some way, they will bind together in a coherent philosophy according to which we can find inner peace. And our rightful place in the cosmos.

And not fall apart, and haphazardly cascade into the chaos of mediocrity before our meditative inquiries like a landslide of boulders sliding downward across the landscape and destroying everything in its path in a mountain avalanche.

Nothing useful can be created from the debris field of that pile of broken and shattered rocks until workers start to clear the debris. And nature then begins the ongoing work of evolution, the process of reconstructing a decayed, disintegrating or destroyed environment. The ongoing work of creation never ends, and we might take that lesson from nature and begin work on the reconstruction of our own false assumptions and failed beliefs.

Life exists on its own terms, not according to the assumptions we continually make and assume to be universal laws. We are the creation, as we know ourselves to be in this present state of consciousness, not the creator. And we should learn to put ourselves in accord with that fundamental realization.

SEVEN

Reconstruction begins

In our best moments, and even in our worst, we often seek some sort of spiritual principle of accord that could offer us the internal peace we seek. Perhaps even without consciously realizing what it is that drives us, we seek the tranquil momentum of harmonic resonance rather than the mentally-disfiguring daily descent into chaos and discord.

Our minds are often consumed by an incomprehensible and incoherent jumble of fragmented ideas, compulsive themes and random memories when we lose ourselves in a babble of mental activity that, of itself, will give us no peace.

And rather than giving us relief from the stress and anxiety of existence, these uncontrollable mood swings only increase the feelings of helplessness and despair that fluctuate within us from one extreme of suffering to another.

The unregulated activities of the mind can become an unmonitored hurricane of activity, and hurricanes generally lead to nothing useful, only death and destruction. This is not a good thing in the overall scheme of conscious living.

On the other hand, hurricanes are also signature elements of the natural landscape, part of the natural scheme of things in the world of material reality. They are expectable, and by analogy and experience, so is the mental discord we will all suffer at one time or another, to one degree or another.

Expectable perhaps, but like nature's hurricanes not entirely happy experiences. These kinds of disasters necessitate that they be attended to before life can move along on a more secure foundation.

Possibly another lesson to be learned from the frequency of natural disasters we experience, either internal or external, along with the difficulties of simply leading a normal human life is that physical existence does not offer us a secure foundation that will always be free from strife.

Life can be wonderful, but none of us get out of it alive. And death, for the aged and infirm, can be the natural, expectable and welcome event that ends suffering in a compassionate way. It all depends on circumstances, and the circumstances all reference the value of relativity.

Whether in consideration of the destruction of the physical environment, or if our mental processes come under scrutiny, we do what we can and what needs to be done to alleviate the suffering that results from unfortunate circumstances.

Except, for many of us, when it comes to the questions that religions raise and haunt our awareness. And the answers that neither satisfy nor complete our understanding of who and what we are.

And especially what we are doing or meant to do here, in this immense and virtually impenetrable cosmos. A strangely incomprehensible reality in which life and death exist side by side, unfathomable sorrow along with the joy of loving relationships and the squeals of children's laughter.

Tragedy and sorrow, joy and laughter all inhabit the same metaphysically-virtual reality show in this universe of physical and psychological duality. What we do and how we do it makes a significant difference of course, but the reality is that duality takes a profound toll on our mental faculties, emotional stability and spiritual forbearance.

Without a genuinely effective method of understanding the inner and outer reality in which we exist, we suffer a potential miscarriage of our best efforts and most worthwhile intentions. The inner turmoil cannot be expatriated by force of arms or wishful thinking. Neither are viable possibilities. The gates of heaven, as such, cannot be stormed and taken by force.

There is only one way to find a safe, secure and lasting inner peace and fundamental accord with the experience of duality. There is only one way, and that is by transcending duality itself. The path to heaven lies within.

Enlightenment is the way out of existential suffering. Not physical suffering, for there is no way to avoid physical suffering as long as we are still embedded in the body. Suffering comes with the territory.

But the interior territory changes when we have gone beyond the mental conditioning that limits our experience of conventional self-understanding, and keeps us entombed on the surface levels of our inner nature. We mistake the familiar mental territory we generally inhabit as the entirety of our inner existence.

But it is not, and that is the fundamental error we have generally been making. We mistake the part for the whole, and judge all that we see or experience only according to the perspective of the part, rather than through the wisdom eye of enlightenment.

This is the error that our spiritual traditions have been focused on addressing, while our fundamentalist religious traditions have generally been intent on pursuing their own agendas, which do not lead to the enlightenment of mankind.

The focus of spirituality is on the education of the spirit, while the focus of religion all too often limits itself only to the education and training of the mind, although it regularly supposes otherwise. But is there really a difference between a supposition and an assumption when neither put food on the table?

The choice a spiritual aspirant must make, when this dilemma is finally recognized, is whether to follow others on the beaten track on their pilgrimage through the forest, or strike out on one's own, without a religious safety net to catch us when we fall.

When we fall we have resource to the sanitizing rites and face-saving rituals of atonement that institutional thinking provides to ease our fall. They often induce a temporary sense of accord when we falter or otherwise collapse of our own weight.

But on a spiritual path we, the collective student, learn to assume responsibility for our failures, and they are understood to be teaching experiences. But not vengeful punishments from a merciless God or incarnate deity of evil.

The trials and tribulations we face here on earth are meant to be, and generally are, the most effective means by which the transformation of consciousness is achieved.

They are the way we are moved out of the stagnation of our mental comfort zones so that evolution can proceed. They are the way we learn on the plane of duality. They represent the interior landscape of learning.

The trials we face, and how we face them, accept them and overcome them are the way the spiritual teachings of transformational processes become inculcated in our thinking and the behavior that follows.

The teachings become effective, not on a one-time only basis, but as a continuing resolution of intent and purpose. And a spiritual training that transcends the temporal difficulties that come our way, and often threaten to overwhelm our mental stability.

By now it should be clear that without a stable spiritual and psychological center from which to act, we flounder along our various paths in life like fish out of water.

The purely materialistic and game-playing orientation some of us follow may lead those without conscience or morality to follow their own path towards the realization of their goals.

Which could mean, in many obvious cases, that there are individuals who will do whatever they want and whatever it takes to get what they want, simply by taking it.

Morality means nothing to those few of us who follow the path of personal corruption. And that is the danger of a culture without a firm spiritual foundation, and a solid sense that personal responsibility is far more than a simple matter of free will and free choice.

Any well-developed and stable mind is perfectly capable of living a moral and conscientious life freed of religious or spiritual affiliation. And history clearly reflects the thoughts and actions of those who lived only according to their personal standards of moral conduct.

But it is probably true that most of us function better and more easily within a well-ordered religious or spiritual framework when dealing with the conflicting demands of a large and complex culture.

Without that continuing and nourishing support, many of us might partially collapse from the internal strains that stress and anxiety cause our minds and bodies to undergo.

Civilization may occasionally have its many discontents, those who experience the oceanic feeling of oneness with the universe, but most of us generally do not have access to that state of security and comfort.

Without the direct communion with a higher state of being we can only hope it exists, and that it is not the symptom of some temporary or permanent psychological disorder. Not really likely, since the reports on that state from those who have experienced it contain nothing but positive and encouraging feelings of bliss and joy.

In generally universal spiritual terminology, one common way that experience is referred to is the opening of the spiritual heart, the spiritual heart being the transcendent center of consciousness within our earthly being.

When the heart opens to the infinite it becomes a gnostic intermediary between the soul and the embedded consciousness. Our conscious awareness is no longer dependent on the rational mind for support and information, along with whatever fantasies it entertains. It is now informed by the transcendent wisdom of our soul wisdom and beyond.

When the spiritual heart opens within us one possible result suggests that we can become transparent to the transcendent. Freed from our bondage to materialistic philosophy, and the pseudo-logical, relatively spiritually-useless and vague theories of philosophical determinism and material reductionism.

Freed as well from the complete domination of the ego that seeks only power and control. And its own shallow salvation by means of the fulfillment of whatever the flowing state is of its wishes, needs and desires. There is nothing permanent or of any lasting value in that. No security, no stability, no sense of the sacredness of life and nothing of the ultimate fulfillment of existence.

This is nothing more than a peripheral state of existential anxiety. It leaves us in possession of little of true value except the satisfaction of whatever fleeting stimulus appears within our awareness and assumes control over our psychological impulse system.

We are no longer in control of our thoughts and actions, our minds and bodies, but controlled instead by the reflexive momentum of unmotivated inclinations and essentially pointless reactionary behavior.

When we find ourselves in accord with this way of being we inhabit a neo-Pavlovian universe of automatic or unthinkingly spontaneous responses. All of them without the redeeming spiritual quality of conscious attention to detail and purposeful activity along earthly or spiritual lines of endeavor.

This kind of existence is a spiritual call and response arena rather than a mental environment of deliberate and thoughtful lines of inquiry along spiritual themes suggestive of transcendent bearing.

Why we should pursue these lines of inquiry is the choice we all must make at some point in our life, or lives, if we hope to continue our evolutionary journey and reach higher planes of existence.

If we are unaware of the existence of techniques for spiritual transformation or doubtful of their value, we have probably not been paying serious attention to history. Or are again, unaware of the inner-teachings that so many spiritual traditions have developed to aid a spiritual aspirant in his or her transformational journey.

These teachings are one way in which we are guided in our evolution by the ability to co-create with the divine in the development and expansion of conscious awareness. We have not been left alone in the darkness that exists under the cloud of unknowing. We have been given the means, the mental means along with self-awareness and imagination, to further our own evolution.

Human evolution was not somehow completed in the only mythical Garden of Eden. Man did not rise out of the physical dust of existence like a medieval golem. Evolution is an on-going process of coming into physical being, and continually refining the result towards higher realms of existence.

Or, when evolutionary progress stalls if the product under scrutiny fails the test of existence, it hangs up a genetic For Sale sign and goes out of business. Or if nature itself, through accident or design, eliminates a failed experiment and sends in a replacement quarterback.

Which could indeed be our fate if we continue on the path of perpetual warfare, mindless consumption of natural resources and the continual desecration of the planet, our only home.

This is an offense against nature, an offense against mindful being, and an offense against the creative intelligence of the cosmos. We did not create ourselves; we are the created and creative product of the evolutionary process.

We should be mindful of that as we go about our daily round of affairs. And we should keep in mind the potential evolutionary advances in human consciousness that spiritual masters and advanced adepts have demonstrated to those who take these matters with profound and utmost seriousness. To learn from a master is an act of infinite grace.

The opening of the way begins when we take our spiritual potential as seriously as we anticipate our next meal, our next endeavor, even our next breath. The inner journey in conscious awareness truly begins when our spiritual evolution is as dear to us as the beating of our heart, as cherished as our most treasured possession, or as precious to us as the health, well-being and active presence of those we love.

It is serious business indeed, but it need not be a solemn and humorless enterprise. If our objective is full consciousness of the joy of existence and the bliss of being, we should begin being joyful and blissful as we undertake the responsibilities of the endeavor.

We need not seek the approbation of those still immersed in the harmful concepts of sin, despair, disillusion and the mounting frustrations of those who have not yet come back to the stable.

The spiritual journey is not one of despair, no matter how many times we may have resolved to do this or that and nevertheless failed along the way to maintain our discipline and continue along the way of our best intentions.

Failure once, twice, three times or more is not failure when recognized as such. They are a multi-varied series of learning experiences that edge us further along the path of self-knowledge. The great Sufi poet, Jalal-ad-Din Rumi made this clear many centuries ago.

> *Come, come, whoever you are,*
> *Wanderer, worshipper, lover of leaving,*
> *It doesn't matter.*
> *Ours is not a caravan of despair.*
>
> *Come, even if you have broken your vow*
> *A thousand times.*
> *Come, come yet again, come.*

Failure is simple another way in which we learn. Even if we fail to achieve a goal, the reality is that we have tried and will again. And the more we *try*, even after each successive attempt fails, the more we will be in a position to finally *do*.

It may take time, but time is what eternity is for. And we have all of eternity, as we return again and again, to finally resolve the issue and consciously make the final journey back to source.

It could be a long voyage, or if we are impatient with the human experience and hope to get on with things we could take charge of our evolution and begin the process of a spiritual training.

We have nothing to lose but the chains that bind us, and the illusions that once sustained us and no longer offer us anything of particular value, comfort or security. The painful part is not so much losing them, but realizing that we have been chained and living under the influence of illusions.

What we truly seek instinctually is concordance with the divine, rather than the familiar and nearly infinite and endless round of internecine warfare between competing religious ideas. Promoted by those who seek the thrill of battle rather than the peace of comity.

Some of us are more enthusiastic about battle than they are about seeking the harmony of existence. They make the assumption that competition is the true nature of the reality in which we live. This belief is what makes it true for them, but not necessarily for others. It is simply another in an endless series of illusions, based more on psychological need, than any corrupted version of eternal truth.

They might consider that mutual cooperation is a better standard of being by which to live their lives, but that requires the willingness to adjust their grasping personal desires to suit the general needs and welfare of the community in which they live.

And this does not suit the imperative needs of those who seek to better their lot by any means available or imaginable. And this is one major reason that many people do not seek to better their lives through a spiritual training.

It is not necessarily that they doubt the truth of the teachings, if they are aware of them, but that they do not wish to change their modus operandi. Fear of change is the enemy, and once again, as always, fear will make an appearance when we are faced with something new.

And this is the value of discontent, when the typical experiences of existence no longer interest us. And we can plainly see through the illusions in which we once believed, and to which we once adhered with a faithfulness that blinded us to the reality of those whose beliefs were different.

Life on the material plane can be wonderful, not only for the thrill of being, but for the possibilities of continued growth in conscious awareness. Once we get past our attachment to physical embodiment, we can learn to appreciate and explore our non-physical existence as disembodied consciousness.

The spiritual journey becomes even more of a challenge, understood more in terms of a precious opportunity to expand our conscious being. To grow in awareness and begin the exploration of additional dimensional realities which we are currently unable to access.

And we can embark on it with love for the enlightened attainments we seek, rather than reacting against life because of the negativity and fear which some religious traditions insist on imbuing in their teachings. They have become anchors around our metaphysical necks.

The spiritual path, in any tradition, is always a path of love, in which negativity and fear have no rightful place. Negativity and fear do not satisfy the spiritual terms of our existence, and do not further our ambitions when we seek the embrace of the cosmos.

We are satisfied with so little when there is so much more available to us. We are spiritual beings who relentlessly deny the eternal essence of our inner being. We insist on playing in the minor leagues of the cosmos rather than moving on into the big time.

There is indeed a big time, and it is where we belong if we will accept full responsibility for the transformational journey. But instead of doing that, we usually only pay Sunday-morning lip service to the divine realm of being.

We are worthy of admittance to the spiritual realm as conscious beings if we are willing to become truly conscious beings. If we accept that status as our genuine potential, rather than accepting the burden of denial that we are somehow inherently wicked and immoral beings by human failure and frequently incomprehensible natural design.

That we are either designed that way by natural instinct, or have devolved from an innocent and uninformed state into the current state of degenerate depravity is absolute and utter nonsense.

Simply an ancient method of spiritual torture used for crowd control, conceived of by harsh and vindictive ancient and medieval minds. As is the silliness of Hell, supposedly a nightmare of eternal punishment approved of by an otherwise loving God. A simply awful supposition, and an offense to our general idea of a heavenly father.

All this having absolutely nothing to do with spiritual training and the education of the soul. But having everything to do with the restlessness of minds seeking control over the lives of others. Misery loves company, they say, and that is often because one can lose oneself in a crowd.

Love is so much more a better and generally more effective teaching than the indignity and shame of preaching sermons that worship hellfire and brimstone as teaching models. And frightening children of all ages.

Who would not be affected when an institution with which we are affiliated considers human life sinful and human beings fallen, in heavenly disgrace, on their spiritual knees and potentially on their way to Hell.

Ouch! That is indeed one hell of a teaching, and a fairly stiff incentive to be good. But it is based on the fear of punishment instead of the joy of enlightenment. And in that sense, as in so many other ways, it is absolutely without merit as an illuminating educational tool.

Any philosophy of life should consider the possible outcome when the psychological drawbacks of its teachings far outweigh the possibilities for spiritual growth. And the overall well-being of the individual congregant.

Most contemporary critics of the religious point of view base their comments on literal and fundamentalist readings of sacred scriptures. They generally tend to ignore the metaphorical implications of what the teachings are pointing toward according to a more sophisticated and enlightened reading.

They tend also not to differentiate between or acknowledge that there are differences between the religious point of view and the goals of spirituality. But there is a difference, and it is profound. It might be said, carefully, that religion is more of an objective point of view, while spirituality is a subjective experience.

The subject deserves prolonged analysis by believers and skeptics alike, and it might also be suggested that spirituality begins, for many people, where religion leaves off. What is loosely termed the religious experience can cover a multitude of relationships, but the spiritual experience is generally considered to be an affair of the heart.

In varying degrees of hope and intimacy perhaps, but nevertheless an opening of the heart that leads inward to a profound state of being. And along the way, an affirmation of life and existence that depends on nothing external for its presence. Nothing that adds to or removes the fundamental focus on the inner reality of divine presence.

For that is what spirituality really is, the acknowledgment of the divine at the core of one's being. And the gentle attempt over a period of time and preparation, through training and practice, to commune with and identify as that inner state. And by doing so, achieving the recognition and self-realization that we are one with the light.

Critics and skeptics should be considering this along with more sophisticated and detailed discussions of the advanced manifestation of the religious impulse, instead of focusing on the most elementary, trite and clichéd aspects of the subject.

This requires more than just a tattered bible to comment on in a grumpy mood. It requires real knowledge of the subject. It demands detailed and intimate study of the history of religion and spirituality, along with the techniques in play that are meant to transform a seeker's consciousness.

And it calls for an understanding of the purported experience of enlightenment according to the words and teachings of those who have attained to it. And perhaps even a willingness to undergo something of a spiritual training themselves, before dismissing the subject as infantile fantasy. Remembering also that matured adults generally do not fantasize in the manner of infants. Criticisms that reel along this line of thinking are the real infantile fantasies.

The subject of religious and spiritual devotion has received prolonged attention over generations and through the centuries. It is a significant dimension of the human experience, and does not deserve to be cavalierly dismissed by adults still carrying a childish grudge, relative beginners in the field and perhaps newcomers to spiritual processes.

Freedom and free will ought not to be exercised in a careless and irresponsible manner. The freedom to criticize without genuine knowledge is unfair and a grievous error, as is the freedom to condemn based on personal prejudice from unfortunate encounters in early childhood, or any other time.

And possibly more generally, the misunderstanding and misinterpretation of transformational teachings due to the lack of adequate study, guided preparation and advanced training. This is not to be taken lightly, or in the same manner as literary criticism.

These are sacred matters, and ought to be treated appropriately, with respect and thoughtfulness, if not reverence. They are the means by which conscious evolution proceeds along universal lines of thought.

Amateur critics, along with amateur criticisms of scriptures dealing with transformational teachings, in conjunction with exaggerated devotional texts misunderstood for their literal value alone, ought not necessarily be taken for impeccable critiques that put an end to the discussion. Satire, they say, is what closes on Saturday night.

They do nothing to end the discussion or bring closure of any sort. They have only the singular effect of focusing their attacks on literal and confusing interpretations of scriptural teachings. And thereby missing the richer metaphorical understandings in which higher values are represented.

There is a sophisticated method of teaching using allegorical and metaphorical images which a conventionally fundamentalist point of view could never be capable of understanding or conceiving. Or if it could, would be obliged by the innate nature of fundamentalism to denounce or condemn it immediately.

That is one powerful reason that fundamentalism insists on a standardized and literal reading of sacred texts, usually presented by individuals untrained in literary techniques other than linear readings.

And because those stories are mistaken for their literal value alone, it requires the invention of miraculous occurrences or an interventionary call on blind and absolute faith to make those teachings palatable.

Which is why amateurs generally miss the point of the teaching or story they interpret only on a literal level. They insist on an either/or focus on existence, which is neither a useful nor accurate rendition of material reality.

It is an eighth grade mentality passing itself off as informed wisdom, when again, it is nothing of the kind. It is a misreading of spiritual teachings, which often depend on intuition and inspiration to pierce through the lowest level of interpretation to reach the higher ground.

The story or teaching must be penetrated by a discerning mind, not relegated to childish babble on a bubble gum wrapper. If that were all there was to a spiritual teaching, the critics would rightly be entitled to their critical field day, even the most ignorant and amateurish among them.

But that is not all there is. Far from it. The literal interpretation is only the beginning of the process. An informed reading leads us along, eventually through a matured understanding to access deeper levels of comprehension and higher levels of enlightenment.

This demands that the student, the spiritual aspirant, adjust his or her conditioned thinking to now move along the lines of the transformational teaching they are undergoing. And to be willing to re-frame their belief system and live according to an enhanced understanding of reality and the nature of existence.

All of this generally involves a near-total reconstruction of whatever world view we have been conditioned by our cultural identities to accept that excludes others of a different identity from our circle of iron. The universe is inconceivably vast, so much so that our small green planet is literally no more than the slightest speck in the immensity of the cosmos.

When we think of the various identities we have assumed, cultural, religious, political or any of the thousand other ways by which we identify ourselves, why in the face of that earthly diversity would we want to isolate ourselves from our fellow travelers upon the difference of an opinion.

And yet we do. So firm are we, or some of us at least, in the settled opinions according to which we express our being, that to conceive of and affirm any identity other than the one we have assumed and developed in our lives could potentially be destructive to our sense of inner comfort and security.

To imagine abandoning that effort and reconstructing our thoughts and feeling along different lines of being, according to a spiritual teaching that asks us to consider what we truly believe, is a monumental effort and truly challenging activity.

An enormous effort of will, heroic really, in that we are striking out for new territory on our own in the virtual wilderness of our unexamined inner life. In effect, a spiritual training drains the swamp within our consciousness, cleaning it of a lifetime of accumulated debris.

These are the memories, dreams and reflections that haunt our waking dreams. They can overwhelm us with a continuing sense that nearly everything we see or do must fit within the various parameters of the forces within us that threaten to pull us apart when their demands are not adequately met.

For many of us there is no central core of authority from which to respond to life when we are so internally fragmented. And filled with existential apprehension at the dawning of yet another day.

We may not acknowledge this to ourselves or others, but we feel it and it works its way into our every thought and action. It can become the tenuous ground of our being if we ignore our inner life and do not take charge of our own evolving consciousness.

If we do not awaken from the virtual sleep of unconscious behavior we condemn ourselves to repeating the same errors of omission that have kept us in the same circular rut we have come to call tradition.

Traditions can give us a sense of belonging to a particular moment in time, and there is a certain comfort in that. But time moves on, and traditions tend to fall behind their moment in the sun and lose their power to inform.

We cannot properly function within the darkness of a tradition that no longer shines a light within us to guide our way. When that process ends, there is nothing to do but reframe our thinking and enlarge our perspective to include the absolute relativity of being.

Nothing in this world is permanent. Nothing lasts forever, and whatever we believe and cherish today will inevitably find its way into our inner storehouse of inert and inactive memories with the inevitable passage of time.

Not even our most firm and solid beliefs will escape the inevitable processes of decay and disintegration. The cosmos is a plane of unimaginable diversity and variety, and our small, green and growing planet in its own way is a reflection of that cosmic reality.

As above, so below is a spiritual refrain of considerable value. A Hermetic tradition that still applies in so many ways, a reflection of the divine within us that mirrors the divine around and above us.

There are two ways of spreading light, wrote Edith Wharton, *to be the candle or the mirror that reflects it.* Another saying that reflects the same idea, and a philosophy that has immediate and practical value.

We may not reach enlightenment in this lifetime or the next, but perhaps there are varying degrees of enlightenment that are still within our reach. Whatever the truth of that may be in our individual lives, we can at least learn to share what we know through our thoughts and actions.

If we are willing to make the effort to clean house and revitalize the inner reality of our being, we earn our place in the metaphysical sun. Heaven is within our reach when we manifest it in our conscious awareness and through our lives.

Fear, when it makes an appearance, will always manifest in some way when we begin a new adventure in life. Every step we take involving change introduces an element of fear. Fear is what we must overcome, not merely the challenges we face, but the fear that attends us every step of the way.

The spiritual path is no different in this respect from any other activity in which we are engaged. We are not disengaged from life when we seek our divine essence. We certainly could not engage in the task if we tried to repress our concerns for our worldly being and earthly responsibilities.

Anything we tried to repress would linger in our subconscious memory and haunt our dreams when we are unconscious and powerless to continue repressing them.

We must face our fears openly as surely as we must feed our hunger and quench our thirst. The ongoing activities of life must be honored and fulfilled while we are still in this world.

To be a monk or swami and live in isolation from worldly activities may absolve us of most earthly concerns, but for many of us the path of isolation would not be the path we choose. The life we are given is the life we must live, unless we consciously choose otherwise on good evidence.

So the reality is we must learn to spiritualize our lives, and reconstruct them along the lines of whatever spiritual authority we choose to follow. Conscious choice is the path most of us take. And what we choose is a reflection of what we believe and how we intend to manifest those beliefs. And there is nothing, absolutely nothing, that is wrong with that.

Free will is the freedom to choose what we will. That is a spiritual Declaration of Independence from conventional beliefs and whatever traditional ties there are that bind. Reconstruction begins when we make a conscious choice, whatever the choice may be.

We are used to authority in our lives. We seek specialists when we have a situation whose resolution escapes us. Medical, legal, educational or otherwise, we generally have no problem seeking and accepting counsel from those who are more knowledgeable and experienced that we.

Where do we go when we are deeply in need of spiritual counsel? There are always the traditional but unenlightened standard bearers, religious clergy and institutional authority. But trite expressions of sympathy, worn-out phrases of featureless empathy, religious clichés or generalized advice we can read in a Chinese fortune cookie have no specific bearing in our lives.

Who can we turn to who has the genuinely earned experience of God-realization and direct spiritual authority? Who and where is the spiritual master whose guidance we seek, but who apparently is not present in the everyday course of events.

And that is the problem we face on the spiritual path, the scarcity of individuals who are truly knowledgeable about the spiritual life and able to help others with the wisdom of transcendent bearing.

The closest any of us might come is a spiritual teaching led by a guide who has been deeply trained in that tradition, and is free from taint and scandal. It is something to be aware of, and the first test of any spiritual aspirant. Discrimination in the choices we make.

Discrimination is not the same as skepticism. To be skeptical is to doubt; to discriminate is to make informed choices, not the blanket hatred of those who act out of ignorance. That is a kettle of fish that has seen its day, a separate reality that does not belong on a spiritual path.

Discrimination as a general mode of being cannot exist in that raw form because it presupposes the value of duality for the individual. Spirituality is concerned to render the oneness of being, the non-duality of enlightened existence, and the unity of being in which we all share.

Anything less than that is not spirituality, it is prejudice. We want to include everyone in our heart-felt prayers and meditations on love. But that does not suggest we must love any actions that separate one from another upon the slightest difference of an opinion, skin color, religion, ethnic group, bank account, sports preferences or bicycle riding.

All that ends at the grave, and it is of the gravest concern that we rid ourselves of those slight and superficial differences and come together as a race of enlightened beings. Anything less than that is unworthy of our attention.

Far-fetched only if our imagination is limited by the contents of our stomach, the state of our finances or any of the mundane terms of our embodiment. How many meals can we eat before the effort wears us out. How many activities can we engage in before they lose their appeal.

When do we finally realize the distinction between our habits and the necessities of material existence. And when do we make a final decision to choose what is best for our long term growth in evolutionary terms.

Which means a transformed consciousness, one that is transparent to the transcendent. A tall order for anyone, but who is there to say that it is not within our reach. *Ah, but a man's reach should exceed his grasp,* wrote Robert Browning, *or what's a heaven for?* Well, what are we waiting for?

EIGHT

What are we waiting for?

Why wait? Why keep postponing until tomorrow when none of can ever be certain we will see the next day, the next week, the next month or even another hour.

Life passes all too quickly when we look back, and time is brief according to mortal eyes. We do not experience eternity, we experience only this moment, remember the last and anticipate the next. Were it otherwise, if we existed as immortal beings our stake in this earthly affair would be far different. But it is not, and time ticks away with a finality that cannot be reversed.

We imagine we know who and what we are, but most of us are unaware of the truth of our being. Our job in this reality is not to eat another sandwich, buy a new shirt or watch another YouTube video. Our job is to realize the potential of what we really are and what we are designed to become.

If we truly believe we were created in God's image, should we not begin our transformational journey by polishing the inner mirror that reflects that image? And kindle the spark of divinity that burns within each and every one of us.

No exceptions to the rule, we are all recipients of the divine bounty. Some of us take it seriously, some doubt, others are indifferent to the whole affair. That appears to be the natural order of things at this stage in our evolution, but that does not suggest it is inevitable that we will continue foundering in our despair.

At some point in our journey through eternity each one of us will come to recognize the fruitless, pointless and dysfunctional pattern into which we have fallen through delay, defer, suspend, pigeonhole and postpone.

Restlessness, negativity and the anxiety that begins when we have lost our energy, our enthusiasm and our zest for the things of this world signal that on a deep, inner level we know we are missing some essential aspect of existence.

Something is lacking, something we can experience that puts us in harmony and accord with the universe in a way that nothing of the material world can offer.

We know this by intuition as well, the realization that time is urging us on towards something new and exciting. Something that will enliven us past the point of attachment and desire, but of a deep inner experience of higher levels of existence.

A distant realm beckons us, not through some sudden anticipation or fear of physical demise, but through an intuitive invitation to enter its previously unknown territories as conscious, self-aware entities exploring the further reaches of mortal existence.

This is the great exploration that awaits us all when we begin to take the spiritual journey seriously. The fulfillment of our religious heritage, the next enormous step forward in our conscious evolution. Co-creators with the divine intelligence. Not as competitive forces of course, but as individual manifestations of the divinely creative intelligence reaching out towards the fulfillment of enlightened being.

What else could it possibly mean that we were created in the image of God according to scriptural injunctions? What else could the divine presence want but that its creation comes into full knowledge of being, and that it achieves the highest order of creative self-knowledge possible. What else could the intelligence of the universe desire but that it be known to itself through the enlightened vision of its creation.

Beyond our limited human imagination, this is what faith and belief are for. To indicate where we should be going and why, instead of as bedrock foundations of the spiritual stagnation that has afflicted us for centuries.

Why wait? Wait for what? For the impossible dream to continue to remain impossible because it is so familiar and so standard an unrealized refrain? And because we have done nothing to actualize it?

How do we justify that spiritual sloth when we look into our inner mirror, and see our reflection moaning about the insecurity of existence and lack of a guiding reality within us to which we can regularly turn.

When we have done nothing to polish that mirror and see what is reflected in it. And which, more importantly, is the very ground of being in which we have our existence. *If only* is not a useful consolation or philosophy when next we lose our turn at bat.

Why wait for that to happen? Why postpone our day of departure from the vague insecurities of unconscious and unenlightened existence to the enlightened perception of our soul's purpose for incarnating on this plane of duality.

We are often held back from the inner quest because some traditions insist that the exploration of our fundamental state of being is not within our purview. Or meant only for specialists with religious titles who hide themselves away from the world and generally keep their discoveries, if any are made, to themselves.

If they have made progress in their inner lives they do not share it, taking refuge in the concept that it might damage their humility. But sharing is not the same as boasting. It is a helping hand, outstretched in the name of compassion.

And more than that, it is a concrete sign that what they have done others can do. We need as many authentic spiritual teachers now than ever before. Not just the revered historical names of saints and sages who lived many lifetimes ago, but monks and cloistered nuns, swamis and yogis. Buddhist, Zen and all other masterful teachers who are alive now, some of whom share their experiences and offer their teachings and guidance.

And that is a wonderful thing, that there are those among us who care deeply about the general human condition. And whose insights into existence are framed in the most generous terms of compassion, empathy and sympathy.

And a firm sense of what we should be doing and where we should be going to enhance our inner state of being. Perhaps not fully enlightened themselves, perhaps more so than we will ever realize ourselves, but advanced enough on the way that what they have to offer can be trusted to inform us in our daily struggles towards the light.

They know the human condition and yet they continue to love. There are beings so firmly established in an enlightened or nearly-enlightened state of consciousness that the actions that wear the rest of us down are of little consequence to our spiritual elder brothers and sisters.

Which is why they can be trusted to inform us. They have already passed through the areas in which we have bogged down. They know the way out of the confusion that settles in and takes possession of our minds like a heavy fog rolling in from a stormy sea and blanketing a coastline.

They have already been there, done that and moved on having claimed their victories over the daily problems that have a nearly unbreakable hold over the rest of us. What they have to offer is liberation, not just from the needs of the body but from the attachments of the mind.

What they have to offer us is the liberation of the spirit as well, free to explore its being without suffering from bondage to any of the conventions that bind the rest of us on the plane of duality. Genuine spiritual teachers are themselves the incarnation of the teachings they offer in human form, with which we can commune.

They are the living examples of those who reconstructed their lives around the opening of the way and the opening to spirit. For us too there must develop a central core of beliefs around which we can build a spiritual system that offers us a firm and solid path over the shaky ground we are treading.

Textbook teachings may be useful and sacred scriptures inspiring, but unless we reconnect with spirit our civilization is doomed. We will inevitably destroy ourselves, as so many past civilizations have done, because we have not a clue what we are doing.

We live in a time when the brilliant successes of technology and science have taken the place of spirit for guidance and instruction. Rational material reductionists have offered an uninspiring vision of the universe in which spirit does not exist, and everything that does exist is either animate or dead matter. In one form or another, matter is all that is, the only thing that matters.

Whatever the cause of animation and consciousness may be, it remains still a mystery to the physical sciences. Whose impulse is to table the matter for further discussion at some unspecified future time. Consciousness does not figure into their equations, yet what else but consciousness matters?

And furthermore, as if to settle the issue, rational skeptics insist that if spirit, or anything connected with it, cannot be measured or reproduced in a laboratory setting under arbitrary controls, spirit is not a genuine phenomenon of life.

But then neither should consciousness itself exist, if physical measurement is the only way life could be judged and understood. This is an absolutely amateurish method of investigating the subject, or of understanding in any useful way the implications of a spiritual realm. And incoherently reaches the extraordinarily meaningless conclusion that spirit does not exist because it is not subject to material measurement.

That kind of methodology is not research, not science, not scholarly thinking, without genuine merit and not worth the effort to voice an opinion. Having already reached the conclusion it originally had in mind, and intent on voicing it without making a serious research effort of any kind, what is the value of such an indeterminant approach?

That kind of thinking had reached a conclusion without any evidence for it other than personal opinion. And slams shut the door to genuine research along spiritual lines of inquiry.

And to be practical about the matter, there is no research funding to be had so why bother about it? And what would be the career goals of anyone inclined to look into the matter, other than an obscure research position in a university with funding to spare?

Who is there to genuinely carry out this kind of research, to be even more practical about it, but the very people who stand most to benefit from a more advanced understanding of consciousness. And more advanced experiences of the depths of consciousness within and available to us all?

They will benefit and learn most who undergo a serious spiritual training, and engage in an authentic meditative effort to penetrate through the various energy constructions of the mind to reach underlying realities.

And each time a new level is reached, to be willing to leave attachment and fascination behind and go beyond even that until our core being has been breached. So we are informed by those who have achieved enlightenment and written about their experiences.

This is an enormous amount of extraordinarily difficult and challenging information to take in when most of us are consumed by the need to focus on our daily lives.

To those struggling to make ends meet it might seem like a fool's errand to devote any significant amount of time and energy pursuing the development of our inner resources.

It might be helpful learn more about the processes of spiritual development before writing it off as a lost cause, but that is in the nature of human development.

We struggle towards the light without understanding where we are going, perhaps even why. But the impulse we follow is inherent within us. The choice of when and how is within our jurisdiction, but ultimately we will follow the light wherever it leads.

We know when we are hungry because we understand the signals our bodies generate. We know we are thirty through similar indications, when we are tired and when we are raring to go. Perhaps the impulse towards the light might be described in terms of human psychology as the impulse towards fullness, towards completeness of being.

It may be that when we are ready to advance our spiritual interests the urge to move forward begins to manifest in various ways. Often proceeded by a sense of malaise that things are not as they should be and the problem needs to be properly addressed.

It might appear to be a feeling as powerful and influential as hunger and thirst, although it does not result from the physical needs of the body. It results from the need of the spirit within us to open the mind and educate the ego with an enhanced perception and experience of reality.

Nothing we can eat or drink, or buy at a convenience store will ever satisfy that yearning other than a profound shift in consciousness in pursuit of the light.

Not that this is a new idea, but that nothing new ever comes along without pushback from established and entrenched forces. They will always be determined to resist change of any sort when it interferes with their proprietary rights and interests in the discussion.

The challenges we face in the matter of spiritual transformation have as much to do with a fundamental lack of support from social and religious institutions in our experiential spiritual education as the expectable difficulties we will inevitably encounter in the transformational process itself.

But not simply a lack of support or educational information, but active opposition to any form of self-knowledge that does not fall under the totalitarian decrees of established authority. As if they who have no experience of the transcendent could possibly have an experientially informed voice in the matter.

In the sense of traditional religious education and conventional belief, we may well be very much on our own unless we seek the support of spiritual communities, support groups or informal gatherings that follow a spiritual teaching or teachings.

We may or may not be individually fortunate in that regard, but there is always the possibility that when enough people become actively aware of the wretched state of our collective spirit, a permanent change in our collective consciousness will be mirrored in our earthly activities.

We can only hope that this will happen in our lifetime and our immediate environment, and the good news is that it is already happening. Not fast enough surely, but change in this regard is more than simply in the air, it is all around us.

Just not enough of a change, but the basics are in place for a collective revision of our religious assumptions and spiritual beliefs. The subject clearly needs to be given more serious attention in the public arena than has previously been achieved.

Anything that contributes to the further education of our spirit in spite of our social conditioning has the potential to free us from the collective burden of conventional thinking and traditionally assumptive thinking and behavior.

Most of those tools of social propaganda do not stand up well under intense scrutiny or the public gaze, but run for cover instead and seek shelter under the misleading umbrella of religious faith or the false flag of a cryonic belief system.

Neither of which can be brought to life in this current day and under these current situations. And never could, not in any other day or any other situation without the support of contributing or associated institutions. And the weight of an armed militia that follow their morally blind marching orders firmly in step with official decrees.

The institutional collective is impersonal, can be immoral, and usually follows the beat of a different drum than the rest of us do as individual souls. They follow the path of power, but as individuals most of us are powerless in the general scheme of things.

The contributions we make might be insignificant in that regard, in the context of wealth and power, but among ourselves, as a general population intent on achieving a more enlightened understanding of our being, we, the people, can be a major force for genuine change.

Social revolutions come and go, and are usually intent on changing the mechanical face of a society or country through changing the nature and management of its institutions and beliefs. Corruption almost invariably follows.

But the movement from religious belief to spiritual belief is a different order of change, and influences the soul of a culture. And that goes deeper into the heart of the human experience than a simple change in leadership, political philosophy or economic management.

The quality of the evidence from the lives and teachings of spiritual masters demands that we pay serious attention to what those highly-attained beings achieved. This is beyond the ability or intention of institutional thinking to achieve, which is why the responsibility for transcendent transformation belongs entirely to us. And will either rise or fail depending on our individual efforts.

There is most probably no other way, not from our YouTube space brothers and sisters, not from drugs or shamanic brews of unusual potency, and certainly not from wishful thinking whose philosophical premise is based on an *if only* mentality.

Action, not daydreams, will achieve the success we hope for. Action is what is called for, and those who imagine that spirituality is opposed to action in the field of physical being have mistaken action for violence.

Only the establishment and those who subscribe to its demands are threatened by change. And yet change is a regular and normal feature of every generation. And every generation resents in turn the challenge to its authority and belief structure that succeeding generations represent.

The universe itself is in a constant state of change, despite the supposed and observable regularity of many of its habits. And if we are to put ourselves in accord with the larger reality the cosmos represents, we should learn to adapt ourselves to the psychological nuisance that there is nothing eternally constant in our universe but the unpredictable regularity of change.

This is the way things really are, and there are ways our understanding and experience of life can improve if we pay attention to the way the universe actually works. Not by decree but by process.

We have the inherent ability to find our place in the cosmos, rather than continue to suffer in the extreme isolation that alienation from source subjects us to.

We can do this if we stop fixating our attention only on those small details of existence that temporarily appease our appetites and anxieties. They may offer us a safe port, for a relatively few hours, in the stormy seas of life. But in the long run they are only finite measures of uselessness.

We can adapt to change, rather than reject change through our psychological autonomic reject system. That part of our being that imagines that the way things are now is the way things will, or should, always remain as long as they work in our favor. But seldom do.

That is simply fear making its regular appearance as we keep our appointments with destiny And we can do without it if we are so inclined. If we are not we will succumb to its entreaties, and if we do we will always live in fear.

We can be shepherds or we can be sheep, warriors or peasant-slaves, carriers of the light or blinded in both eyes and suffering throughout the remaining sunless days of our existence. The choice is always ours. Free will again.

There is nothing permanent in life, nothing, nothing, nothing. We cannot hold fast to anything, not a physical structure, not a substance, not an idea, an emotion, not even our bodies.

We can hold on to nothing in this life other than a firm and unshakeable identification with the underlying consciousness of the universe itself that resides within. Our divine nature, which precedes and succeeds our physical existence.

Our original face, that which we wish to regain, and truly speaking already are if we will get off the merry-go-round of unconscious existence and allow our inner nature to manifest.

We have built our homes on sandy soil and shaky ground, and they will tremble, shake and fall apart when a strong enough wind comes along to blow them down. Anxiety, stress and fear are hurricane-force winds that threaten us on a near-daily basis. When we retreat into the relatively fragile ego-structures we have built or allowed to develop within us we are not living on a safe and secure basis.

Nothing will afford us that security if it is not allied with the universal force of existence. And if we continue to deny the existence of that divine presence we will never establish a secure inner connection to anything, substituting instead the insecure continuum of our fragmented thoughts and shifting feelings.

We could learn to trust in our own instincts in those solitary moments when we sit back and reflect on the cosmos and our place in it. We could allow ourselves to think deeply about the matter without editing the process and our feelings. We could examine our feelings carefully, in great detail, even more than our thoughts on the matter.

We could allow our instinctual, intuitive wisdom to seep through the mental filters we erect that prejudge our thoughts and feelings. And then dismiss whichever expressions of our being do not fit comfortably within whatever the particular mood of the day may be.

Intuition may not always be correct or reliably dependable, but sometimes it may not be the voice of intuition to which we are listening but ego mistakenly believing itself to be a higher source of knowing when it is not.

When we learn to recognize the genuine appearance of intuitive understanding, free from temporal desire and material attachment, it is a source of knowledge and wisdom that can lead us out of the frustration of ignorance, out from under the cloud of unknowing.

If we are clear enough we can find our way through the mental debris field in which we are sometimes immersed. We have the means within us to find our inner light. And if our intention is strong enough and our willpower adept enough to enforce the power of intention, we may secure that inner connection with great regularity.

To which we may always have continued access, and thereby learn to take an easy detour around the roadblocks that life will always throw up in our path. It's not personal, it's just life going about its business.

Sometimes we just get in the way, but we are part of the flow of life. We stream through existence as surely as a mountain brook flows downward from its source into the ocean of existence waiting below.

If we dam our outward expression of being through rigid adherence to a concretized series of man-made rules of existence, we tie ourselves to the fashion of events that have seen their day come and go.

Last year's fashions have seen their day, and live on only in short-term memory. We will not see their likes again in our voyage through time, except in museums devoted to past achievements or in moments of nostalgic yearning.

We can admire the past but we cannot live in it, not now, not ever. Our independence from past conditioning is not really a choice, it is a necessity. We cannot live today according to yesterday's demands or last week's needs, and we will not be able to live tomorrow by slavishly following only today's beliefs or the state of whatever contemporary knowledge is yet to come.

Life changes too quickly to rely on outdated information or ideas that have outlived their time. Life is always in the process of evolutionary change, and so are we, but not necessarily always in the sense of enlightened presence.

We may change on a regular basis, but that does not suggest that we always change for the better. Only that we change. Changing for the better unconditionally demands we assume control of our evolution along enlightened lines of thought and feeling.

And that requires us to assume conscious control over our evolution in regard to the understanding and experience of our internal states of being. We ought to learn something of what that means, of course, and that is when we must turn to our spiritual history to learn what has already been accomplished by those who led the way.

Prejudice, superstition and the intimidating experience of learning a new vocabulary could present occasional obstacles. But they are insignificant unless we succumb to their reactionary and strangely intimidating negatively-inspired blandishments.

The educational alliance between religion and spirituality may be threatened when new ideas or strange concepts, usually only familiar to advanced practitioners, make their sporadic appearances and threaten the stability of the worn-out playing fields of religious sensibilities.

We may be striking out for new territory in the expansion of our conscious awareness, but there is also reward in the challenge of exploration and the learning experiences in the journey towards wholeness.

That expansion of consciousness is a door that not so unexpectedly leads to other doors, and those in turn lead onwards to infinity. The game we play when we do that is of profound consequence, not something we do for material reward or earthly advancement.

In another sense, according to some spiritual masters, leaving the physical realm with the enlightened awareness of a transformed consciousness has been compared to escaping from central prison. Prison being the enforced confinement of an enlightened consciousness within the limitations of a physical body.

What that could mean to those of us who appreciate being within the confines of a human body seems impossible to conceptualize. But then, most of us believe that we are only our bodies. And we are incorrectly informed by rational skeptics with medical degrees, but no proof of their claims, that consciousness is merely an epiphenomenon of the human brain.

Spiritual masters, on the other hand, thankfully teach the opposite of course, that human consciousness is eternal and immortal. And the evidence for their claims lies in the extraordinary abilities they demonstrate, hearsay to those who have not looked into the matter but gospel to those who have.

It is an attitude not easily dispelled or disputed that the loudest and most vocal critics of the abilities displayed by spiritual masters have not themselves looked seriously into the subject of spiritual transformation and what that implies.

Beyond criticizing biblical miracles and the shallow claims made by religious con-men, material reductionists have generally contented themselves with feeding at the trough of religious skepticism and superstitious disbelief.

Superstitious because many of them have turned from the creative and infinite spirit of the universe to the rational exegesis inherent in the semi-mystical and magically-inspired belief that human reason and mathematical logic alone can unveil the secrets of the universe.

What they have achieved is a continuous and advancing understanding of the mechanics of the physical realm, but nothing of the spirit, or intelligence, behind it.

But then again, conventional religious traditions have not added a great deal to the mechanics of the discussion either, mysticism aside. Most religions have contented themselves with ancient beliefs, stagnating when it comes to further discoveries of the spiritual realm.

This is a terrible error, for religious authorities should primarily be concerned with advancing the cause of spiritual enlightenment. But most are not, seemingly intent instead on hogging religious territory with imperialistic designs that to those with a broader outlook do not appear to advance the cause or interests of sincere spiritual seekers.

More than just regrettable, it is a glaringly-outstanding indication of where we have stalled in our evolutionary development. That those who should be most involved in the evolutionary thrust of our spiritual interests are not.

They have contented themselves instead with carrying out institutional functions and fulfilling religious duties that substitute the re-enacting of ancient rites and medieval rituals for the ongoing experience of direct communion with the divine.

One argument for this is that people are not ready for more sophisticated and advanced religious teachings, and that institutional authorities can best be trusted in the disposal of the matter. They do not generally advance an alternate explanation for their restrictive attitudes.

The rebuttal for this is the argument that institutional authorities do not have more sophisticated and advanced religious teachings at their disposal. Or that the experience of enlightenment from which to teach is beyond their abilities or formal doctrines.

This is an over-simplification of a complex problem, but the essentials are correct. And it might be an unfair criticism in this regard, for enlightened spiritual masters are relatively rare.

We cherish them when they appear, those who recognize them for what they are and what they have attained. But they represent an advance and an anomaly in human development.

Which makes it all the more imperative that what they represent, the enlightenment of the human species, should be the ongoing research activity of the religious-minded and spiritually-oriented. And with formal academic and institutional support, as well as general encouragement.

Information is out there and available for those of us who hope to reconstruct our inner being along the lines of spiritual enlightenment. Although it would appear that for many of us the subject generally flies below our collective radar.

Why this should be is as much a matter of our relative immaturity as a species, at least according to the re-fashioned norms of the current state of what we call civilization. Perhaps human history has forgotten, misunderstood or is unaware of past civilizations in which a greater and more pervasive degree of spiritual enlightenment was a matter of daily concern.

But it is also true that our religious institutions have failed to adjust their thinking according to the evolving needs of humanity, rather than the enforced propitiation of their institutional presence and power.

And in doing so, in concentrating their overall activities on advancing their institutional foundations, they have failed to advance us as individuals. We are what they ought to be concerned with, not the maintenance and building of architectural monuments to their only-imagined past glories and wish-fulfillment fantasies.

The spiritual enlightenment of mankind along general lines of endeavor, equally applicable to the whole of humanity, should be what *all* our religious institutions are concerned to render. It is what religious thinking ought to be but so often is not. It is what the spiritual enlightenment of our species represents, and is.

The either/or mentality that afflicts our world-wide religious heritage helps secure the well-being of none but those enclosed within their closely-knit circle of indifference, set apart from those on the outside. And should there even be an outside when one is concerned to influence and advance the spiritual activities and well-being of mankind,

The sun, the moon, the stars, rain, wind and air shed their bounty on all equally. How could anyone believe, much less teach, that the creative force of the cosmos prefers this one over that, requires one belief over another, admires and longs for one particular color, plant, tree or song of endearment.

All and everything that exists in form, in objective-reality, exists within time and within the creation. But the eternal nature of the creative intelligence of the cosmos is without form. And that is our true home, the source of being, that with which we are eventually destined to re-unite.

All and everything in this creation is destined to change as long as it is within time. Even our most cherished beliefs, even our most sacred teachings, even the forms of religious practice will eventually change as cultures and beliefs evolve.

We can hang on to nothing but the consciousness with which we are endowed. Which is what we are, the witness-observer of our physical manifestation on the material plane.

When we learn to understand this basic fact of objective-reality, we may find ourselves having an easier time of it when it comes to enhancing our spiritual perceptions of the cosmos.

Perhaps it simply takes time for that to occur, but time is not at our disposal. It is a natural resource over which we have no control. And which cannot be replenished in this lifetime by any means when it begins to run out as we age.

Many of already have attained to this realization, which is not so difficult to grasp when we reach the mid-point of our lives, But which is still difficult to actualize within our psyche. We hang on so desperately to our youth and the physical presence of our being that it tends to blind us to the greater reality.

Or perhaps we simply do not want to see the truth of physical existence that time represents. It frightens us to think that one day we will no longer be incarnated in physical form. Oblivion, if we do not believe in reincarnation, is what awaits us.

But if we do believe, the struggles of re-birth and re-education in a new body, forgetful and no longer able to access the familiar accoutrements of our present existence, is still something of a challenge in longing we may not necessarily wish to endure.

No longer able to fulfill our dreams, enjoy our achievements if any, or share in the bounty of the family and friendships we have created. Much less the material rewards of a lifetime of rewarding activities.

It all ends, all of it, and all that we will ever take with us is the state of our consciousness and the enlightenment, if any, of deeper states of existence. If we have achieved this, moving on will be its own reward.

If we have not, we will depart this life with fear and trembling, which is clearly not the proper condition in which to enter the afterlife. There are manuals of instruction that develop this point in great detail that are available in many world traditions. We might consult them before our time here is over and we move on in darkness rather than in light.

We should avail ourselves of that knowledge before we leave this world, and that might be the most difficult aspect of a truly spiritual training. Besides learning how to live in this existence, we also have to learn how to leave it.

It is certainly an achievement that may unconsciously be what we are waiting to accomplish. But lack the existential nerve to confront, as long as we still believe we have many options left to experience while we enjoy physical incarnation in this world.

Death waits for no man, and death comes when it will and at any time, and always when our time here has expired. Whether by accident, design or due to the natural and inevitable decay of our bodies, we will all one day depart this world and thence comes the unknown mystery we so fear.

If we can learn to overcome our fears and forego our attachments we will leave this world in good standing, able to move further along in our journey through eternity. If we do not we will return, perhaps in a newer and improved form, but perhaps not. In one sense the decision may be ours, but in another, perhaps it is not.

If we have done our best here to advance our spiritual interests we may see the rewards of that manifest in a happier and more fruitful incarnation. It might even be that there might not even be the need or desire to reincarnate.

Perhaps the challenges of existence on a more advanced plane of reality are far more desirable than the experiences of physical reality alone. That is something about which we can only speculate without advanced knowledge, but the possibilities of that existence certainly can excite our imagination.

Material reality has its rewards and its drawbacks, but we are here and here we stay until it is time to depart. We could consider using some of that precious time to consider our options concerning the afterlife. And just as in any other course of education, prepare ourselves for graduation.

Where we go, what we do, how we do it and why is not even properly a matter for speculation. Where would we begin, and what information do any of us have to inform our concerns.

Not much, only hope and the faith that, according to the teachings of highly attained individuals, we do go on. And that is well worth whatever time we spend in researching the topic, calming our fears and readying ourselves for a change in location. Once again, what are we waiting for?

NINE

Calming our fears

Many of us have a great deal of trouble controlling our various appetites. The various degrees of interests and addictions we entertain in the market place absorb a good deal of our attention, if we cared to take a few steps back and think about it.

Surely those things cannot be what existence is about and life is for. Food, clothing, shelter, material goods, mind and mood-altering substances from tobacco and beer to more sophisticated means of altering our internal processes are by-now normal standards of behavior, many necessary of course.

But when they run the whole show, when they become the reasons we continue to inhabit these bodies and do our best to live lives of infinite material pleasure, something has gone amiss in our very souls.

We are on the wrong path and we know it. Something inside us knows, our conscience certainly when it responds to the foolish activities to which we have been giving uncritical attention.

And then overdoing what began as an initial diversion from the temporary stress of a gloomy day. Now made permanent by our inability or unwillingness to avoid resorting to addiction as the solution to our problems.

But our spirit suffers, and the constant presence of suffering is reflected in what some of us experience as an indeterminate malaise that seeps over whatever remains of our internal core of being.

Lost in that inner fog, some of us fruitlessly scramble to sort out the details of our life, until all that remains of our efforts towards internal house-cleaning results in massive failure and endless frustration. This can lead to nothing useful, only more of the kind. And as long as it continues, our consciousness will be tediously aware of the inner fears that plague our being.

Some of us know fear as intimately as our very breath. Breathing is usually beneath our conscious level of attention, but fear is not. It captures the spirit. We take our breathing for granted, as though it was the normal, natural condition of our lives and we need not pay it any serious attention.

No so with fear. It infiltrates our being and settles into the very pores of our skin. Every move we make takes into consideration the fear of something in our movements. Every thought, every impulse, every decision reflects the fears we have sheltered within our being, and welcomes them into the intimacy of our decision-making processes.

Even our breath, of which we generally take no notice, reflects the mechanical hesitancy that fear creates. And who among us has not noticed the shortness or quickness of breath from which we suffer when we are afraid.

We all know fear, and for good reason. There are many things to be afraid of in this life, and part of our growth and maturation is learning what those things are. And how to deal with them, or if possible, avoid them.

On this plane of duality love is as much a part of the scenario as fear. The duality of existence. Love and fear, attraction and repulsion, expansion and contraction. For every action, there is an equal and opposite reaction.

Love has its own scenario in its various manifestations, as does fear. Which has the deadlier consequences when it goes astray is a moot point, but fear, when it settles into our spirit can end or retard our evolutionary progress.

On the other hand, love tends to encourage the evolutionary thrust of being. Not always, but often enough to make love a valuable ally in our experience of material existence. Exceptions abound of course, but which would we prefer when we have the choice.

Perhaps love is not love when it moves into emotional extremes, but something else, closer to an addiction. During the average course of events, we would probably all choose love according to the general human attributes pouring forth positive and life-affirming energies. These are usually not present when fear overcomes our senses.

Fear clearly does the opposite as a general state of psychological imbalance. If a hooded cobra slithered up to us, reared its head, bared its fangs and began hissing we would most likely all feel fear. And rightly so.

But when we are not immediately faced with extremes of physical danger or mental distress, but live in an unspecific state of fear and internal disorder, help may not always be on the way unless we have regular access to a paid professional.

When we turn our attention to what a spiritual path represents, and what we are obliged to permanently set aside in our journey towards the light and the genuine rigors of the voyage, we may begin to feel the effects of fear for any number of honest reasons.

Our addictions and attachments divert so much of our mental and physical energies to the satisfaction of their demands that the constant drain they represent usually presents a major obstacle to our meditative focus.

They are always somewhere on our minds, in the forefront of behavior or in the background, as a distant or inactive memory. Ever-ready to spring into action, we may generally find ourselves unconsciously holding back in anticipation of some spontaneous urge that threatens our impulse control.

Unmotivated fear accelerates the ways in which we hold ourselves back from direct, forceful and holistic action. Nothing so much degrades our humanity as much as the deliberate and fearful withdrawal of our conscious energies and our presence here in this earthly realm.

An existentially unmotivated fear of existence haunts our being, scattering our attention in a thousand directions. And so to gather our internal resources with a laser-like focus on our inner being may be, for many of us, an unreasonable expectation and impossible demand.

This is when we can take the support of a spiritual teacher and a spiritual teaching. And begin using whichever of the various methods the teaching has developed to help us focus our mental energies on whatever task is at hand.

If a teacher is available, we have the guidance of an experienced hand to help us choose which technique, or sequence of techniques, would most likely produce the most beneficial results.

If a teacher is not available we simply begin at the beginning and continue from there. Unless fear takes a hand at the table and influences us to question our choices, the technique, the teaching, or even the viability of what we are trying to achieve in the first place.

This is most probably inevitable for many of us, and might be considered a natural course of events for beginners, especially those with a general tendency towards skepticism and denial.

Skepticism and denial might be useful tools in their own right, but they lose their emotional appeal when one begins to make progress on a spiritual path. How to define useful?

A brief return to Hamlet would be useful here. Hamlet is not a coward, but he has lost the courage to deal with life on its own terms, not his. He has lost touch with the central core of his being. He no longer knows what to believe about anyone or anything, and consequently lacks a psychological and spiritual center from which to act.

Without that center of psychological attention and core values of spiritual belief he is unable to bring his plans, such as they are, to the fruition of direct action. And on the material plane, direct action is not an abstract philosophical dilemma, it is the result of a basic question of identity.

A problem that Hamlet cannot resolve because he questions his very identity, until a series of extraordinarily miraculous occurrences affirms his recognition that there is meaning and order in the universe according to a divine influence.

This he believes with his whole being when the realization finally sinks in and permeates his consciousness that *there's a divinity that shapes our ends, rough-hew them how we will.*

He is now free to act, freed from any existential anxieties that withheld his attention from his responsibilities. And consequently accelerated the fears that lead him to question even his own identity. Hamlet is alive and well though, and living within us all.

We all question our identity one way or another, and the answers that come our way may often be based on whatever role we are playing at that particular moment in time. We enact the personas of the various roles we play in life with specific details that turn an archetypal performance into performance art. And the yogi, they say, is the artist whose greatest work of art is himself.

But we are not those roles, nor the characters we create, and when we question our true nature and spiritual identity, if we do, things may not work out well when the roles we play do not hold up well under the pressure of intense scrutiny.

We cannot uncover much of lasting substance or sustenance by identifying our essential being in terms of earthly phenomena. Neither social, business, political, philosophical nor any other category of being. And not by the clothes we wear, the food we eat, the groups we join or the individuals with whom we associate.

They are not our true being, none of them, and will fade into memory with the passing of time. Whatever role we play today will end when we assume another role tomorrow, another identity, then another and then another. That is the game of life, and the theory of reincarnation adds additional dimensions of being to the mixture.

We often cannot find the truth of our existence when we identify ourselves only according to the necessities and obligations of material existence, the temporary or short-term functions we carry out in the general course of our lives.

When powerful moments of introspective analysis occur with that famous shock of recognition, we may find ourselves opening to the existential anxiety and immobilizing despair that so often comes hard upon the loss of a secure personal identity.

A strong, healthy and vibrant sense of being, empowered by a strong ego-centered awareness can help us ward off the approach of the existential angst that makes freedom something to be dreaded rather than embraced.

Even so, our fears will eventually find a crack in our internal armor, and often begin to surface beneath our conscious attention until they explore with a volcano-like force that threatens to overwhelm us and withdrawal our attention from active participation in the world.

As long as we rely on the surface features of our existence to protect us from the essential fear of simply being alive and vulnerable in a physical body, we will always be subject to the unknown and incontinent terrors of the night.

But as Buddhist teachings maintain, we must actively participate in the sorrows of the world. Although many of us never do forthrightly address or insecurely deny the existence of the anxious thoughts that rise up from the subterranean nightmares of the dark night of the soul.

They haunt our memories like shadow figures flitting about on the internal screen of our awareness, first here then there, but never exposing themselves to the full light of conscious scrutiny.

And that is our doing, for it is within human nature to find a multitude of ways to avoid, escape, censure, deny and repress any thoughts and feelings that do not comfortably empower whatever particular fiction is concurrently being employed and embraced.

The melodramas of our lives are uninterested in critical analysis or formal investiture in the embrace of consciously-functional power and authority. They are dreams we are acting out, not reality.

And we know it. They are temporary experiments in being, often acting out on impulse what under different conditions might otherwise have remained merely an idiosyncratic daydream. We are trying life on for size when we do that, and then rejecting the unfinished products of our imagination.

And we often have much, if not everything, invested in maintaining them until the energy that empowers them has run its course, or been replaced by a more powerful impulse seeking physical expression.

That is the very problem that is the cause of so much of our anxiety. We know deep inside our being that whatever games we are playing are all eventually fated to run the course of their existence. They are temporary situations, subject to the exigencies of time and fate, as ultimately are we.

Fear has a physical as well as a mental dimension of being, but existential anxiety is a wholly internal set of circumstances that presses its weight on our conscious decision-making processes with results that are anything but imaginary.

Fear of any kind can turn us into calcified stone, and existential fear can act from within to petrify our imagination and turn us into emotional zombies and energy vampires. Feeding on the energy of others when we cannot find the power of existence within ourselves from our own resources. We allow fear to dominate the conversation and sometimes even rob us of our instinct for survival.

Fear may be a natural instinct for survival in a hostile environment, but it is not the natural condition of our soul, which knows no fear. Nor need it be mistaken for the natural condition of our spirit, our hearts and minds.

Fear need not become an essential ingredient of our psyche except if it should infiltrate our psychological make-up and takes up permanent residence. If it does and becomes powerful in its own inner circle of influence, we may become unaware of any alternative to the desperation of fear's embrace when we are caught up in life's struggles.

We may be caught in the spider's web, but there is an antidote to fear. And it is not only within our grasp, but the essential and natural condition of our minds and hearts when they are attuned to our soul presence.

When we are one with our inner self and in accord with our fundamental nature, the bliss of the universe is what we experience because that is what we essentially are. We are the blissful awareness that fills our inner being as it manifests in this world.

When we turn to our spiritual heart in the embrace of love we open our being to the bliss of existence. We open to the radiance of life, that which the creative spirit of the universe yearns to express and experience through its various manifestations. Ecstasy, rapture and bliss, the joy of existence.

Any informed spiritually-enlightened psychological stance suggests that the most profound experience of existence we can ever hope to have is when we open up to the radiance of life. Anything less than that is simply psychological reductionalism limiting the scope of our imagination and attention.

We cannot take in more than we can see, and we cannot hold on to more that our peripheral spiritual vision will allow us to grasp. Our spiritual faculties and human imagination will apparently always be limited by the energy we direct into the process.

Focus and concentration, rather than wishful thinking and idle speculation, will help direct our attention where it belongs if we intend to make progress on a spiritual path.

All spiritual teachers direct us to this most difficult task of building our spiritual confidence based on real results. Picture books and entertaining tales based on archetypal religious themes and imaginative stories are useful and pleasant ways to encourage children.

But at some point in our inner journey towards the light many of us outgrow the playthings of childhood and embark on a path of genuine and specific achievement. Do we not already know this, and if so, why do we continue adding to the retinue of the artifacts of spiritual materialism?

They entertain and amuse us, those toys of childhood, but when childhood ends many of us will painfully awaken to the realization that their real function has been degraded if we have continued relying on them as adults.

Their usefulness as artifacts of spiritual enlightenment has ended, and the continued reliance on outdated methods of understanding and worship have led us only into the trap of spiritual stagnation which we cannot easily avoid and from which we cannot easily escape.

The familiar and addictive intercessionary mediations between man and spirit have diverted us from the painful process of ending our total identification and affiliation with the material plane of being.

We must learn to stop thinking of ourselves on the human level as separate from the cosmos, and recognize that we *are* the cosmos. We are not *in* the creation through our human incarnation, we *are* the creation observing itself through the human template.

And most importantly, the culminating experience of our human identity will be to surpass the human identity itself and move up on the evolutionary scale of being. To attain the self-realization that our eternal spiritual identity is the Self of the universe. And nothing less than that sublime reality.

This may be something that frightens some of us and intimidates others, possibly because we will have to relinquish the limitations of materialistic belief systems if we are bound to a spiritually-oriented but self-deceptive system of duality.

Which means undergoing the withdrawal symptoms that a path of spiritual enlightenment will force us to undergo, however gently the process, as we ultimately embark on the transformational process.

But what we can achieve will offer us a natural and far more infinitely rewarding experience than what we are leaving behind. We outgrow everything that comes our way in the human experience. But unless we remain attached to our behavioral and psychological habitual patterns of behavior, we can leave them behind with the freedom that comes about with the release from any addiction.

Difficult to think of the human experience as an addiction, but from a more advanced evolutionary point of view, we are chained to the body, embedded in the physical, and attached to the material plane.

We move on when we are spiritually, psychologically and philosophically ready for new experiences. But until we are, here we stay and here we burn when we enter the psychological domain of existential angst.

The way out is to live according to the radiance of spiritual existence, within Agape, the unmotivated spiritual love that inflects our experience of this world when we allow it to enter our awareness.

When we open out to the radiance, the radiance of the divine will change our experience of reality. This reality is an experience, not the permanent dimension of our being. We assume differently because we constantly judge what is real only according to our physical senses and material standards of measurement. And we often judge wrongly and prematurely when we do that because we base our judgments on incomplete and inconclusive evidence.

This leaves no room for the non-local dimension of being as it exists in itself, or as it intercedes in physical reality. What some of us refer to as miraculous occurrences may be just that, the intercession of the spiritual realm into our material experience of being.

How that happens, why it happens, when and by whom or what it happens is a subject worthy of the most serious attention. But that it does happen is beyond dispute if we will listen to genuinely informed authorities.

We could all be informed authorities ourselves if we will turn to the spiritual realm with genuine seriousness of intent to access the information and guidance that is always and ever available to us.

No need for gnostic intermediaries of any sort who claim the territory for themselves. Religious guidelines may be helpful and are often necessary, but the power to turn within and find the inner reality that haunts us belongs to each of us, alone and apart.

We are each of us responsible for our own evolution. No organized institutional authority exists that can move us an inch closer to our spiritual goals unless we ourselves are willing to do the inner housekeeping that can free our spirit and what lies imprisoned within.

And that is the task before us, to free ourselves, our real selves, from the cycle of continuous incarnation in the physical. And then move on, our spirit free to access higher realms of conscious, self-aware existence.

The experience of higher states of being is what informed the founders of the great religious and spiritual traditions. But institutional authorities who declaim their passions in the name of those founding masters, long after religion became established and organized along hierarchical lines, do not seek to empower the individual congregant with the same potential ability as the founder found within himself.

Instead, they seek a master-servant relationship with the divine, respectful certainly, but still disempowering the spiritual seeker often to nothing much more than a whimpering, original sinner-based mentality that freezes the soul in suspenseful terror of the unknown. When religion follows this path it is on the road to an evolutionary dead end. It is not spirituality, it is superstition.

And this is where spirituality begins its ascent. When a spiritual seeker longs for the experience of religious fulfillment for himself, within his own being, the institution to which he looked for guidance may no longer be able to fulfill that deeply personal role. The power and guidance he seeks is within, and turning inward is what he will do. Male or female, it makes no difference.

When the individual desire for truth and the direct experience of the spiritual realm overwhelms all other concerns, overpoweringly direct and personal, the subjectivity of spirituality will often replace the objectivity of religious institutional thinking.

The yearning for a direct relationship with the divine can be so self-empowering and self-fulfilling that an individual willingly takes on the direct responsibility for his or her spiritual education.

The purpose of the religious impulse does not lie in obedience to the central commands of some external force or institutionally-appointed authority, but in finding the source of all authority within one's own being.

The only sure and certain antidote to the existential fears that fill us with anxiety and a subtle dread of life, and what next may come, is the radiance, existential closure and spiritual certitude that the genuine experience of direct contact with the divine offers.

That is the path, according to those who for one reason or another, whether through practice, preparation or what some might call divine grace, have declared has been their experience.

Science has nothing to say about the experience of enlightenment since it is clearly not within their jurisdiction, Strangely, religion also tends to discount the experience of enlightenment unless the experience is framed well within the parameters of its specific traditional dogmatic beliefs. As though God could be bound in a nutshell by those who have bad dreams.

The problem with the material reductionists, in this regard, is that their reach far exceeds their grasp. Which, unfortunately, has not succeeded in hindering them from making detrimentally-exaggerated claims about religion for which they have no evidence.

And which is also not supported by bombastic utterances, all sound and fury, but signifying nothing. Rational materialists have cause to criticize many religious traditions and many religious beliefs, but it is only established religions with fundamentalist orientations they attack.

Never do they attack spirituality or mysticism, although they are both tarred by the same brush. And never do they even mention spirituality or mysticism. This is a curious omission from their general rules of censure, but there may be a reason for it.

Most rational materialists and material reductionists who have staked out a public position in the general attack on religion almost always fail to discriminate between religion, spirituality and mysticism. As though, in the absence of all but religion in their general censures, they are each of them referring to one and the same thing.

They are not, and that is perfectly obvious to any informed observer. And that is precisely the problem, for they are not informed observers. In their own fields, perhaps so, but spirituality and mysticism are clearly not within their specific field of expertise, if any, and they are not therefore knowledgeable enough to hold informed opinions.

They simply have opinions, and they are strong opinions, voiced loudly and frequently at the top of their lungs. And often tinged in aggrieved tones of personal injustice. Emotional, exaggerated and pulsing with subdued anger, as though perpetually reliving injuries they may have suffered many years before when they were children and have not been able to overcome. Who can tell.

But still, this is a general problem associated with a cerebral-based culture. A civilization that imagines it has created itself, that the universe is here only to serve mankind and in turn be despoiled by man at his whim. With no laws in sight and no convictions to be obeyed.

As he imagines himself to be at this stage in his evolution, cerebral man thinks himself fit, capable and carries a self-imposed and self-authorized mandate to re-order the creation in accordance with his own terms of reference, being and behavior.

In a sense, we are fishing for minnows in the vastness of eternity. Who could even begin to imagine the cosmic intelligence that has fashioned the universe against which we, even at our best, are simply minnows ourselves swimming in concentric circles that diminish and close in on ourselves as we begin to age and wither away.

So much easier to simply deny the existence of any intelligence greater that our own, and inscribe our own names to the authorship of the creative process. So much easier than for material reductionists to acknowledge that their knowledge and understanding of creation is limited and flawed. And that the spiritual realm, which they deny exists and which is anathema to them, is the true source of creation and human existence.

As though no creative divine reality was the power behind creation, primarily because science has not discovered a way of measuring and replicating God or the creative spirit in a laboratory setting. The part that pretends to be the whole cannot see through its limitations. As though a minnow could measure the ocean in which it swims, or even imagine the vastness in which it and it's ocean exist.

Religion partially addresses the issue by concretizing a subservient relationship between man and the divine, which in one limiting sense is true. But spirituality attempts to bridge the gap between existing spheres of influence by reconstructing an individual human life in terms of surrender to the divine reality, in all our terms and methods of activity.

Mysticism attempts to achieve identity with the divine spark within us all through merging individual identity, body, mind and spirit, into the divine reality. The only way the minnow can know the ocean is by becoming the ocean, and the only way to do that is to stop imagining that it is only a minnow.

Something that many of us are reluctant to do, much less conceive of as within our human possibilities. There is safety in being a minnow if we can avoid the dangers posed by larger fish. And seek shelter in the anonymity group culture offers. Some of us are perpetually content to remain within the school of minnows in which we swim.

If we remain within the lesser flow of a group mentality, we may never have to consciously face the existential questions of being which the group mentality occasionally and from a careful distance addresses. But will never be able to solve through a conscious encounter with source.

In spite of the restrictive and fearful mentality that denies rather than investigates the spiritual origins of the universe, the hyperbolic addendums that substitute for informed experience will never do to further a progress. Or jumpstart our evolutionary progress when we have stalled.

Only when we open out to the radiance of the sublime spirituality of our inner selves will we ever find the enthusiastic energy to add to the spiritual momentum of our progressive evolution.

Thinking man must evolve to become spiritual man. We must evolve, and open up to the inspiration and guidance of the inner radiance of spirit, rather than rely on our mental faculties to inform our being.

This is a serious blow to the collective ego of cerebral-man, but what choice do we realistically have as we see the works of thinking man descending into chaos and corruption on a world-wide scale.

If we can learn to observe this realm of material existence with truthful eyes, with insight and intuition, it would be difficult to avoid seeing that civilization is approaching something that feels very much like some great force of expansion is nearing an end. A traditional way of doing things perhaps, and perhaps a fundamental change in the way we do business is in the processes of growth and maturation.

Whether that change is simply putting a newer face on older forms of corruption, or a radical realignment of our conscious being entwined with and informed by the underlying spiritual basis of reality, is the problem to be dealt with.

That change may be something that will benefit the whole of humanity, or benefit only a select few of the empowered, is also a question we must all inevitably address. We can be part of the change or part of the problem, or we can content ourselves by swimming along in relative anonymity in whatever direction the group flows. We may find ourselves feeding on plankton, or being fed on ourselves.

But if we do nothing as a collective force we lose our chance to create change and inscribe our own names in history. Nothing will change except the skillful ways in which the empowered few and their hired enforcers take advantage of and control over the mass of humanity.

We, the people, no longer a force of conscious destiny but destined instead for disposal by those who believe the creation belongs to them, and is their rightful property to dispose of as they will.

Unless we oppose them, and seek the internal empowerment which is rightfully ours. Any group effort towards the realization of a collective goal demands a powerful force to hold the disparate currents within it together.

The natural individual impulses of self-identity threaten to tear any group effort apart unless some common goal or force of identity emerges from the chaos of the social mass.

Considering the reality now that the entire planet is in peril in so many ways from so many sources and directions, the only source of power to which we can actively turn has to consider the whole of creation in its activities.

We can no longer shut our metaphysical eyes to the real world around us. We can no longer rely on some newly-fashioned political appeal that as in all such attempts is laced with internal cyanide and built on quicksand.

If we want real change in the way our world is run that change will have to come from within. The salvation we yearn for will have to work its magic within our essential being.

The rules to which we will voluntarily adhere in this brave new world to come will have to originate from the unmotivated love that lives within the spiritual heart. To which we all should look to inform our being without regret or the eventual necessity of consolation.

Our thoughts and actions, as we go about the business of the day, should have their origins in the same inner reality in which we all share our fundamental being. That is the force that will bind a world-wide effort to change the corruption that has become so continually present in the halls of power.

It may be a force of collective adhesion, but it will only come about, if it is to be genuine and of long-lasting duration, through individual effort. We each must take the responsibility of becoming spiritual spelunkers within the depths of our psyche.

When enough of us have ventured inward and found the same inner reality, and then compared notes in public forums for others to see, we will begin to trust the obvious changes that must be put in play.

When enough of us have had the same or similar inner experiences we can trust that they are authentic and genuine to our inner state of being. And that being the case, the walls will come tumbling down and we will begin to build trust in one another.

Differences may still remain, but those differences will be on the surface of things, not representative of any unacknowledged inner agendas that in truth, will no longer exist with the same force of being as they do now.

A true concordance with our inner being can potentially bring about a genuine concord with others who share in the same experience and attainment. We are all brothers and sisters, not enemy agents skirmishing in anticipation of a broader encounter.

Our very lives are on the chopping block when we are at war, with ourselves and each other. Only our shared humanity, at its deepest and most profound levels, is capable of leading us out of the darkness in which we dwell and are collectively leading our lives.

We are a species perpetually at war with each other, and extinction cannot be very far down that evolutionary dead-end unless we find the will and the way to divert our thoughtless and deadly momentum and choose a different evolutionary path. A distant realm awaits us.

Any contact with the bliss of being, the inherent legacy of the human experience of the spiritual realm and our collective inner reality, is most likely the only force capable of thwarting the spiritually immature and reckless impulses so many of us demonstrate that can only lead towards mutual destruction.

Without doubt, we are surely heading in the way of mutually-assured destruction through one disaster or another. The only difference it makes in knowing how we might potentially destroy ourselves is in finding a way through which we can counter its momentum.

We must take arms against a sea of troubles, again as Hamlet postulates, before those troubles overwhelm and destroy us. As always, the only time in which we can act and act effectively is *now*. The *now* moment which is the only moment in time in which we *can* act.

We can put that change off no longer. The air is polluted, as are the land and seas. Where else is there to light out for new territory, only to soil whatever nest we imagine we might temporarily inhabit there.

There is nowhere else to go on this planet that the hand of man has not already reached and demonstrated the carelessness of his ways. We should be ashamed of our stewardship of this planet and many of us are, in as public a way as possible.

But we have polluted our souls as well, as long as we remain content to live only within the confines of our minds and egos while avoiding any meaningful encounter with the truth of our spiritual hearts.

Enough, surely, is enough when the planet is imperiled and survival itself is on the line. After so many lifetimes and centuries of internecine warfare and endless struggles, isn't it finally time to re-evaluate the way we think and behave along different lines of endeavor.

The Shangri-La of our existence, the inner peace and outer harmony which we hope to secure for ourselves does not require a change in location. It only requires a change in perspective, and a willingness to search within, the only place in which it can exist.

There is nothing to fear, nothing to lose and no harm to be endured if we are willing to change our fundamental ideas about life. We are far more than we imagine ourselves as being, and to settle for so much less than we are capable of achieving seems to pollute the very concept of human progress and evolutionary advancement.

Mystics and advanced spiritual adepts have seen the future in this regard, and reported back through their presence and teachings, and often enough the miraculous interventions from the spirit realm that accompany them.

They represent a major thrust in our collective evolutions, and they inhabit a more highly evolved stage of being than the rest of us. We ignore this at our peril, and what is it we can be so proud of that we have substituted for the reality of peace and harmony that they have achieved within themselves.

Nothing so much in terms of an average human life and the general condition that humanity endures. Scientific progress apart, some of which when devoted to the armaments race has done little to advance our interests if we wish to avoid wholesale slaughter, cannot truly be added to the rolls of human accomplishments of long-term and lasting value.

Long-term value is what we should most be concerned with, the survival of our planet, our environment, and life in all its multiplicity of forms. Nature has not selected for extinction the many of the life forms that have, until recently, shared this existence.

We have, through our carelessness, greed, and our indifference to the bounty of sentient life forms. Our own survival is at stake as well, our children, grandchildren and all others who swell the ranks of the human family.

It is our family as well. We all belong to it and one another, and we should find within that which assures us that our separate reality is, in reality, only one.

Ten

We all belong

The universe is our home, the Earth our birthplace, and we all come from the same divine source of all being. There are no heavenly deities, good or evil, fighting it out for disputed territories, perpetually at odds with each other and often enough with us as well.

We need not fear. There are no fiery habitations created for eternal punishment as well, and no angelic beings floating in the clouds on gossamer wings with harps always at the ready for musical encounters with like-minded entities.

We all belong here, children of the cosmos and we all have the same rights of full citizenship with equal shares in existence. We need not fear eternal punishment from a wrathful deity with an uncertain temper, and any book of rules and regulations rigorously enforced whose violation dooms the willful or ignorant trespasser to genuine terror.

This is a concept of universal spirituality that belongs to a formidably antique vision of creation in which enforced discipline through occasionally harshly over-reactive injunctions pre-dated the opening of the spiritual heart as a more effective way of regulating potentially unmanageable human behavior.

We might honor the necessity of mediating the unregulated passions of ancient eras, for we ourselves may not be all that dissimilar considering the constant state of warfare that rules over a great deal of the environment.

But considering the mystical teachings of truly advanced human adepts, that antique vision of creation may need updating along more fruitful lines of endeavor.

Heavenly reward is certainly as much of an inducement towards virtuous behavior as the fear of Hell. But in this our technologically advanced world is Hell really a valid concept in the same universe as an eternally loving heavenly father.

Not the reward of some vague eternal existence playing harp in a heavenly choir, or any such similar nursery-school nonsense. And not the abstract reward of having lived a virtuous life while denying all human passions.

But the transcendent reward of having advanced our human interests in the incalculable immensity of the universe. The reward of becoming more proficient explorers of conscious existence. The reward of expanding our experience of consciousness itself, of unfolding our creative abilities through the transformation and transcendence of mundane consciousness.

The ultimate reward of becoming far more than simply a 'lumbering robot' following automatic and pre-determined tendencies in a mechanical universe, but of becoming co-creators within the divine imagination.

We do not have to justify our existence through artificial means of endeavor. We justify our existence by existing according to the fullest possible dimensions of our being. Body, mind and spirit are the three dimensions of the human experience which are the natural territories of our explorations.

We begin with the body, move on to the mind, and then incorporate the spiritual dimensions of our inherent being, which remain yet to be discovered by the unenlightened many, into our mode of existence.

This is what makes humanity an unfinished work of art, an experiment in being in which human evolution is still subject to the ongoing activity of creation. Creation does not simply stop at the physical or end with the creation of planetary systems. And whoever said it did.

Creation is the on-going activity of the unknown source of all being, whatever name we might individually want to call it. What difference could a particular name mean when we are essentially all referring to the same mystery of existence? And yet, to many of us a name makes all the difference in the world, but none at all in eternity.

Only the endlessly futile and petty attempts to define the essentially indefinable, and the follow-up rules of order and regulation instituted by institutional-minded men make the difference between one set of religious beliefs and another.

Less worthy of attention than a straw on a camel's back, but with the same power to command attention when men fight over the fall of a sparrow as significant of divine propriety.

This has given rise to anti-religious attitudes over the centuries, resulting in this day and age in the abuse of religious authority to maintain and enforce demonstrably-flawed belief systems. Along with the antagonism that should be directed at flawed humanity misusing spiritual traditions, but is aimed instead at the infinite spirit of the universe. An easy target, unless one is on one's death bed.

When free will is used in our favor it is celebrated as a gift of grace. When it is used against our interests we claim it is misused, and then condemn the creator for bringing a flawed concept into existence.

But we usually do not condemn a cow when a baby spills its milk, or tweet our displeasure at three o'clock in the morning when it rains and interferes with our plans for a week-end. Some of us, at least, have developed more matured restraints than giving in to erratic impulses at all hours of the day or night. Or succumbing to unmodulated behavior in response to the petty grievances that enter our awareness from time to time.

Free will allows for the extremes of behavior the human species exhibits when emotions and intellect roam over the full range of thought and feeling. Our activities reflect those activities as well as our freedom of choice.

But is it not also true that for most of us the choices we make reflect our understanding of the human situation and the problems we encounter in dealing with it. Add to that our desire to improve our lot, increase our wealth, insure our health and well-being, and secure for ourselves a solid and secure base of operations in this world of change and duality.

A tall order, considering the temporary length of our earthly stay, more like a short-term visit to a planetary theme park than a permanent place of residence. And difficult if not impossible for most of us to accept considering the unknown territory that lies ahead of us when our bodies are no longer adequately functional and capable of sustaining the energies of life.

But here is where we are, here is where we belong, and if we can accept our embodiment in these physical bodies as our rightful place in creation, *we might then also begin to have faith that what comes next, whatever that might be, is just as rightfully ours to experience.* Our heritage goes beyond our functionality in the material realm.

The limitations of the body do not change the fundamental nature of who we are as conscious, self-aware independently-existent entities. We confabulate the two, and identify only with the physical because of the unrecognized inability to experience more than just our conscious ego-driven existence.

Consequently we suffer from those physical and mental limitations as well. Not simply that, but also from the failure of imagination that results in an individual and collective group-failure of nerve. We deny ourselves the fulfillment of our spiritual potential because so many of us cannot see any further than the tip of our nose. Or want to.

But one day we must all prepare ourselves for our eventual departure from this existence, and with the fullest possible attention to detail. Along with a rejuvenated belief system that incorporates the same faith in our spiritual, disembodied future that we have in the present. And had when we were young, free from cynical pre-determinism, and believed with the innocence of childhood.

Cynicism and greed, combined with the emotional void of material reductionism, have had a severe effect on our hopes for the future. Not only for ourselves, but for the planet and the very purpose of physical existence.

If we believe what we are told by rational skeptics, we really have no place to go and nothing to turn to when we consider the causually-unknown nature of our existence. A spiritual realm which we are informed by material reductionalism does not exist, based on no proof other than their highly-prejudiced personal opinions.

Science this is not, although it is passed off under the general aegis of scientific progress at the expense of spirit. Personal opinions aside, we need far more than that when we consider our fate and general well-being.

But anyone pretending to speak from earthly authority about spiritual matters ought to have genuine mystical experience to back up their claims. And without resorting to dogmas, rites, rituals, or references to ancient books and quotations from medieval scrolls to prove their case. The hard facts of the matter should be reinforced with serious and successful ventures into the depths of the human psyche, producing results that verify their beliefs.

We need a more sincere and profound vision for the future, not a sentimental but backward glance into mythology mistakenly revered as direct revelation.

And not attained from bilateral excursions into memory and imagination involving antagonistic elements of the ego and mind involving the pseudo-spiritual realm. That is not spiritual knowledge, it is the mind confabulating with itself and interpreting the results according to the emotion of the day or the mood of the moment.

The facts of the matter are often considered to be in serious dispute when we have only the pleasant poetry of ancient books and medieval manuscripts to lean on or console ourselves in times of trouble. Spiritual knowledge and direct experience is a far better way to nourish our being when stress and anxiety come knocking at our doors.

We might genuinely prefer a method for consciously entering a state of mystical enhancement ourselves, or so some of us might imagine in those moments when we are alone and considering the matter in the dark of night.

When we cry out for help, and no one is there to heed the call, it does not signify that we are alone and without the comfort of spirit. It suggests far more than that if we can separate ourselves from the pain of earthly existence.

It suggests that it is time for us now to turn within, and there find that same inner source of strength and power that sustained our great mystics at the moment of their greatest need.

Every religion and every spiritual tradition can provide the details of those who suffered on their own crosses. And something of the means they had at hand, as far as we can know, to overcome earthly peril and function on an exalted level of spiritual identity.

This does not mean the end of suffering, it means the end of our attachment to suffering. We, the spiritual witness within, do not suffer. Our bodies suffer and so do our minds. As long as we are remain attached to physical incarnation, this is always the way it will be. It comes with the territory.

But as we are informed by our spiritual teachings, those of us who are listening with genuine attention to detail, we are neither the body nor the mind. As long as we believe we are we will suffer. The transformation we undergo is more than simply a change in our belief system, it is what we identify ourselves as being from the experience of higher consciousness.

For those of us who really are listening with genuine seriousness of attention, this is more than just a comforting thought in times of need. It is the way out of suffering, the way out of anxiety. It is the opening of the way.

The way does not lead to a sublimely hidden castle housing spiritual truths, spiritual artifacts and spiritual beings somewhere in the outer world. And protected by magical spells, armed guards, a surrounding forest housing elves, dwarfs, ghosts, goblins or fairy queens.

All those are simply fairy tales. Charming, adorning, embellishing and illuminating the imagination of the lower self, but only metaphors pointing out that something glorious awaits us all. But the direction is not somewhere out there in the world. Nowhere and nothing is to be found in the forests and jungles of the material world that can offer us inner illumination.

The true direction is within, past the barriers the mind and ego erect. In reality they are merely monuments to earlier stages of our conscious-awareness, and they are self-protective.

When we come into true knowledge of our inner being it becomes crystal clear that our existence is a temporary phenomenal stage of awareness on the way to self-realization. When we realize that the way to enlightenment opens.

We have stagnated in our spiritual evolution because we have always relied on the functionality of the human brain for knowledge of this world and how to live in it. Never realizing, during the course of an average human life span, that through self-realization there is a better way to obtain information.

We need to repair the damage we have done to our earthly affairs and soul presence, and embark on a teaching that illumines the way home. Enlightenment is what awaits us, our true home and the royal road to self-knowledge.

Once realized, all distractions fade away and lose their power to inform our minds and control our destiny. Confusion, anxiety and the despair of meaninglessness and meaningless activity become what they always were to the inner spiritual witness of our ego/mind orientation.

Nothing so much becomes our humanity than our leaving it for the greater glory within. A heart-breaking departure for those who are not ready, which is why they are not called, or if they are, do not heed the call of the epic voyage to the spiritual heart.

But to those who are ready to begin the adventure, spirituality is a journey through the inner wilderness that leads to the Promised Land. The voyage to sacred territory is always within. Even the thought of any piece of real estate as being more sacred than any other, having more spiritual power than the plot of land upon which we are now standing, becomes just another illusion.

And as much of a distraction from the sacred task of self-realization as anything that takes our attention away from the self-recognition of our inner being. It is not the intelligence of the mind and the ability of the brain that will lead the way in this adventure, but the intelligence of the heart that seeks its own true domain.

The heart has a voyage of its own to make, the escape from the spiritual restrictions of the lower self. The three stages of love is an exploratory journey from infatuation to attachment to universal love by way of the unmotivated tenderness of the heart.

Eros is the first stage the physical being experiences, concerned as it generally is solely with genital energy and sexual attention Eros is the lustful attraction of the physical for the physical, and the energy of Eros remains stagnated at the level of the sexual organs.

Amor is a higher stage of the attraction of one being for another. Not the opening of the spiritual heart, but the opening of the human heart. The attraction of one heart for another, one to whom the eyes, as was sung by medieval troubadours, have opened to the heart. Eros rests with the sexual organs, Amor resides in the heart.

There is an even higher stage of love, the highest known on the material plane to human consciousness, and that is Agape. Agape is the experience of universal love without conditions, without motivations and without limitations.

Agape is spiritual love, the spiritual intelligence of the heart. Unfolding the love of the creation for the sake of the creation, for the benefit of all being, under all conditions of existence and all orders of experience. The underlying order of all dimensions, all realities.

Agape is the love of the creator for the creation as evidenced in and experienced through an enlightened heart. It is the final goal of the evolutionary voyage through all human states of emotional expression, and the ultimate leave-taking of lesser forms of emotional forbearance.

When we live in a state of Agape we live in harmonious accord with our emotional and mental states, and the rest of creation. This again does not suggest that we can avoid the sorrows of the world, only that as we now know ourselves to be, in accord with the state of enlightened self-realization, we do not suffer. We will feel pain, but in the enlightened state we simply observe the experience. Pain will still hurt, but we are not the pain.

This is neither psychological detachment from reality, nor self-deception in a hypnotic-like state of waking dream fantasy. The way out of suffering lies in transforming our consciousness to attain a higher state of conscious existence, self-knowledge and self-realization.

The reality of earthly existence does not preclude this achievement, it is an achievement because material reality is the test we must overcome to enter the greater glory of conscious illumination.

The question of identity will only be fully answered when we have attained to the plenitude of all human possibilities. We are meant to overcome the individuation of separate consciousness that has succumbed to material illusions, delusions and self-deceptions.

And during that process of self-discovery become transparent to the transcendent. To function in accord with the divine reality within us that is our true nature, and our true identity. We only imagine that we live in a separate reality, apart from the divine injunctions to *Be!*

To question that divine ordainment, *Be!* may be the genesis of our spiritual learning experiences as the meaning of it unfolds over generations of experience and lifetimes.

But when we have learned the lessons of lifetimes of individual earthly experiences, when we have attained to an enlightened state of any degree, our questioning responses to the divine commandment can only be a very humble *Let be!*

When we accept the gift of life and the bounty of existence as the gift of a benevolent creative force seeking only the expression of its being in manifest existence, we can turn within with the assurance that, as Dame Julien of Norwich so confidently maintained, *All shall be well, and all shall be well, and all manner of things shall be well.*

This may not be within our immediate power to grasp with the fullness of our spiritual intelligence and identity, but our spiritual identity is what we should truly be questioning above all else.

Who and what we are ought to be the focus of our serious attention under the terms of any system of self-scrutiny. Our present being is a causal function of our soul, our personal past in this lifetime, and in previous but unremembered lifetimes as well.

Perhaps there is also a relatively odd possibility that what we call synchronicity or meaningful coincidence may suggest a past or future lifetime somehow influencing present-day reality Which may or may not be simply fantasy, or might imply that time is non-linear, and could have different trajectories in different dimensions of existence.

Whether or not that is a real possibility only time and break-through discoveries will tell, assuming future generations make significant progress investigating the nature of material reality. Perhaps science will one day ally itself with what is currently denigrated as a mystical and therefore non-productive approach to the physical world.

When science recognizes that consciousness, not matter, is the fundamental building block of the universe, that alliance may become a working partnership. When individual scientists recognize from their own experiences that mysticism and spirituality are not fantastical religious mumbo-jumbo, serious research might begin.

Mysticism and spirituality offer a working method for understanding material reality and what lies beyond this dimension of awareness in their own right. Add this to that, the successful conclusion of any experimental attempt at transforming consciousness could result in an expanded consciousness with extraordinary abilities to affect material reality.

This is one area of fundamental agreement between science and spirituality. In science an experiment is carried out under laboratory conditions to achieve a desired result. But the scientific method is not confined to scientific investigation and scholarly researches alone.

The very same principle is just as true, and just as profoundly practical, responsible and offering genuine results by following a spiritual tradition. The desired result of any spiritual teaching is the direct and subjectively-undergone experimental observation of consciousness, and the unveiling of profound inner states of being and what that implies.

And the result, if the training a spiritual aspirant undergoes is successful, is a transformed and expanded consciousness capable of achieving both mastery over many conditions of material reality and conscious awareness of and entrée to the spiritual dimension. In this sense, an enlightened consciousness might well become an inter-dimensional time-traveler.

This also suggests that the attainment of spiritual mastery informs that individual awareness of the unaffiliated truth of being. Which is why we trust the wisdom of an undisputed spiritual master with the fullest confidence that our trust will not have been misplaced.

This puts us in a difficult position, those of us who are involved with reality. There is so much in life which requires us to judge one thing over another that a firm and solid knowledge of reality is an absolute necessity for our continued existence and the achievement of our evolutionary goals.

But what in our knowledge of the physical world and material being qualifies us to judge the spiritual attainments of a spiritual adept of high standing. How can the lesser judge the higher? Nothing in this world prepares us in the standard course of events for any encounter with the unknown reality of the spiritual realm.

This is certainly why viveka, or discrimination, is one of the earliest requirements of any beginner's inquiry into the metaphysical world of spiritual reality. It is a fundamentally causal function of a penetrating intelligence, which in one aspect is a requirement for self-realization.

Not the only one to be sure, but a crucial start to any investigation of the inner life of mankind. There are many ways of re-connecting with source, and whichever one is appropriate for any one individual is the proper path for that person. The sun shines its light equally on all.

There is absolutely no need for anyone to compare or contrast one path with another with a view to judging others, which can only lead to blind judgment and hateful discrimination. The world has seen enough of that since our tribal days.

But we live in a world community now, and there is no going back. The Internet has made it possible for people to connect from every corner of the globe, and the dissemination of competing ideas and personal opinions cannot be stopped without harsh and overt censorship.

When it comes to our spiritual identity, the proper study of our religious and spiritual heritage ought to automatically include all of us, cultural differences aside and totally irrelevant. In our fundamental nature we are all of a piece.

The self-serving mechanisms of prejudice, bigotry and intolerance by now should be seen for what they are, the childish emotional manifestations of immature and conscienceless individuals intent on preserving their local territory for themselves to the exclusion of all else.

Immigrants from any culture or mind set are unwelcome in that reality, as are all who display any differences that set them aside from the local group identity. It is the wrong way to look at things, and an incompetent way to live in a global environment.

We should be celebrating those things we all have in common as spiritual brothers and sisters, rather than condemning the slight differences that set us apart as individuals. And those differences ought to be celebrated as well, as reflections of the creative intelligence of the universe, providing they do no harm to anyone else.

There is power in diversity and joy in the infinite variety of the creation. It should be clear by now that diversity and variety is in the natural order of things, in existence long before mankind decided to re-order the universe according to its own scattered plans for creation.

We should be in accord with that creativity, not intent on re-structuring existence according to whatever irrational impulses infiltrate our awareness. And thereby destroying the harmony of existence with our separate plans for a separate peace.

There is no such thing as a separate human reality, and no amount of restrictive alliances intent on preserving the bounty of existence for the favored few against the disenfranchised many can disrupt the essential underlying harmony of the cosmos.

The harmony of existence is where true power lies, once we learn to tap into our deeper roots. The authenticity of our racial identity is as individual incarnations of the divine creative impulse to be.

It is that within ourselves with which we should be in accord. That with which we should identify. That according to which we will continue to evolve in alignment with our true spiritual identity.

The most pressing question that must be answered is not who, or what, or where, or why. The question of identity that must be answered now is *when,* and the only answer to the imperative urgency of that inquiry must be *now.*

The *now* moment is all we have, and if we do not make use of our opportunity to evolve and take charge of our own evolution we will lose it. And we must fight, not only to preserve our true heritage, but to incarnate within us the dormant flame of spiritual harmony.

Someone, something or some process will begin, if we do not seize the moment, that will retard our evolutionary progress in some monumental way. Progress always comes at a price. Conservative or reactionary forces will always feel threatened when change appears on the horizon, threatening their world view and the territory they inhabit. They will act to preserve their wealth, status, power and privilege.

And when some natural or man-made disaster overcomes the front lines of civilization, back we will go to the caves to start all over again. Only this time without the natural resources we have now so remorselessly depleted that once sustained us in the past. And facing the slow spread of a nuclear alert that may well destroy the planet.

Anyone with eyes to see and ears to hear can recognize the signs of a civilization that has reached a breaking point. We are threatened on all sides by the collapse of civilized world cultures, and the inherent dangers of a world in which violence is the chosen method of communication. Frustration with the world as it is has replaced all manner of civilized discourse.

We can do better, but too many of us throw our metaphysical hands in the air. And protesting their innocence, proclaim in ringing tones that the system is broken and cannot be fixed. And when they say and believe that they are right. The fix is in, and they have nailed it to the cross.

We have stagnated in our extraordinarily flawed stewardship of the planet, as well as in the exploration of our inner being. Content to stay where we are, looking after only our individual needs and desires, we accept the frustrations of daily life as though we are powerless to change anything.

But we are not, and we ought to take our clue from the universe which is in a constant state of change and evolution. Change is the natural order of things, and one must either evolve according to changing conditions or fall behind and face eventual extinction.

Life does not come with guarantees. If it did we could cash in our chips and move on to something else. But that is not the way things are, which we know but keep in reserve in the back of our minds as though it actually was a possibility.

Drugs, alcohol and addictions may temporary quell our fears, but the world we enter when we succumb to our fears is of no lasting value and no material benefit, and can do nothing to improve our earthly lot.

Artificial inducements are not a source of power, they offer nothing but illusions and a temporary respite from fear. The true source of power lies within, and we have been told that for millennium by our spiritual traditions. It has apparently fallen on deaf ears.

We have ignored the message. We have chosen the way of material obsession, as though the accumulation of goods and services, useful in our earthly existence, will be enough to satisfy our earthly conscience and spiritual well-being when the time comes that we leave all this behind.

When our time here has expired, and we must move on to the next stage of our being, all we will take with us will be the transcendent wisdom of the spiritual heart. What that leads to may be unknown in the present stage of our existence.

But if we are going to publically maintain a belief in an unseen God, perhaps we ought now to take advantage of the full message and prepare for what next may come. We may not know what lies around the corner, but it is inescapable that we are heading in that direction.

When we have reached the point at which we realize something fundamental is missing in our allegiance to and appreciation of earthly existence, we may find the courage, energy and the time to begin the exploration of our inner being. Explorers of the universe, are we, and spelunkers of the psyche.

If we are confused about ourselves, our identity and the rightness of our being we should remember the simple reality that we absolutely belong here. This is home, this is where we should be and here is where we are meant to expand our being. And then we will move on.

And because we all belong to the universe we belong to each other. We are all family. We are all united in the struggles and successes of earthly existence, and can find shared comfort in the reality of material being.

There is no comfort to be found in the despair of existential angst, or any such failed philosophy of existence. There is no point in throwing in the towel and retreating to the fog shrouded never-never lands of alienation and isolation.

We do not have to be alienated from life. We do not have to be in isolated from our fellow men and women. We do not have to lead lives of quiet desperation. We can find hope and the bounty of existence by living in and acting from the treasure that is our spiritual heart and spiritual being.

That is what we have always been and what we will always be. Spiritual beings temporarily incarnated in physical form. Forgetful of our original nature and hindered by the burdens we have assumed by separating ourselves from the source of all being. All that ever was, all that is and all that will ever be.

This is the truth of our existence, and the claims of material reductionists that deny our spiritual nature lead nowhere but to the metaphysical grave. We are more than merely an epiphenomenon of the brain, and whoever thought that one up should go back to the drawing board.

The brain is simply the incredibly complex receiving biological mechanism through which consciousness manifests in physical reality. A receiver and transmitter of information, and our bodies the vehicles through which our souls experience the unfolding realities of material existence.

And share in the bounty of existence, adding whatever it may be we are each individually capable of creating. We are more than the world, more than our various cultural contributions, more than accumulators of goods and services and occasional dispensers of some portion of what we have earned or inherited, to either hoard for ourselves or share with the world.

We are individual sparks of the divine reality, individuated aspects of the creative intelligence behind the universe. We are the children of the creator in a dualistic sense, but in a non-dualistic view of reality, we are the very universe itself awakening to its existence as sentient, self-aware life forms.

In that we should rejoice and end the foolish habit of isolating ourselves from each other and alienating ourselves from the universe. Separation from source through individuation does not mean we cannot continue to affiliate ourselves with and act from the inner bounty of a transformed and enlightened consciousness.

What other treasure do any of us have that can compare with the depth, power and richness of our inner being. Nothing in our earthly experience can compare with the experience of God-realization, self-realization, self-recognition, self-actualization, or any term we may use to describe the process of enlightenment.

That is the ultimate solution to the question of identity in this world of duality and constant change. The only answer that fully allows our inner being to manifest is enlightenment. Enlightenment is the only answer that empowers our internal processes of self-recognition, clearing the way for the continued evolution of our soul.

In every sense we are the world, we are the universe, we are the divine consciousness of the universe coming to know itself through the forms that have evolved to allow the divine to fully participate in the bounty of its creation.

The divine is always present, and always available through its presence if we will only look where it truly dwells and may be found by concerned seekers. Because of that we are at home and at play in the universe. And whatever comes our way is always and ever simply the play of consciousness.

◆

ABOUT THE AUTHOR

Louis Rogers was the host and producer of the television interview series Turning Inward, and the founding publisher and executive editor of Inner Paths Magazine, both in New York. He was also the founding publisher and executive editor of Pir Publications and Sufi Review located in Westport, Connecticut and New York City.

Professor Rogers began his career as an instructor at Hunter College in New York, then turned his attention towards publishing spiritual teachings. He has written numerous books, articles, editorials, book and magazine introductions and prefaces. His short story, The Zhikr of the Heart, first appeared in the London-based magazine, Sufi Journal.

In 2001, he returned to university teaching as an Adjunct Professor in the Department of Languages, Literature and Media Studies at Sacred Heart University in Fairfield and Stamford Connecticut, and later as an Affiliate Professor at Fairfield University, also in Fairfield, Connecticut.

His previous books include: Ladder to the Sky, an adventure novel set against a modern and mythological background of Taoist energy teachings and legends. Coming Alive: Accessing the Healing Energies of the Universe, Mirror of the Unseen: The Complete Discourses of Jalal al-Din Rumi, The Fire of Love: The Love Story of Layla and Majnun, Call and Response: The Wisdom of Rumi, The Age of Spirit, Tales of Immortality, What Do You Expect God To Be?, Where Do We Go From Here?, Bridging The Gap, Who Do You Think You Are?, Kissing The Spider, That Which You Wish To Be, What Next May Come, The Face In The Mirror, Rebel In The Mind, and most recently, A Hand In Time. A Question Of Identity is his nineteenth book.

Made in the USA
Middletown, DE
04 March 2017